Strictly Come Dancing

Strictly Come Dancing

Rupert Smith

Dance consultant: Len Goodman

BBC
BOOKS

First published in 2005 by BBC Books,
BBC Worldwide Limited, Woodlands,
80 Wood Lane,
London W12 0TT

ISBN 0 563 52293 3

Commissioning Editor: Nicky Ross
Project Editor: Helena Caldon
Designer: Bobby Birchall, DW Design
Production Controller: Kenneth Mckay
Step-by-step dance photography: GMK

Set in Minion and Frutiger
Printed and bound in Great Britain by CPI Bath
Colour separations by Dot Gradations Ltd, UK

Picture Credits
© BBC Photographic Archives for pp9, 13, 114,
118, 122, 126, 130, 134, 138, 142, 146, 150

© ABC Photographic Archives p13
(Evander Holyfield)

All other photographs © BBC and © BBC
Worldwide Limited

BBC Books would like to thank photographers
Rachel Joseph, Gregory King, Trevor Leighton,
Keiron McCarron and Abi Wyles

Contents

Foreword

W hen I first heard about the idea for *Strictly Come Dancing*, I fell about laughing. My manager and I had been taken out for lunch by the BBC, who wanted to discuss a few formats with me, and when they mentioned this idea for *Celebrity Come Dancing*, as it was then called, we laughed and we just couldn't stop. Jane Lush, then controller of entertainment, looked a bit worried and said, 'Are you laughing at us – or with us?'

The truth was that we were laughing with them – it seemed such a fantastic idea, something that had been missing from television for so long, and we were relieved as much as anything. I told her I was definitely up for it.

Strictly Come Dancing was just what Saturday-night television needed: something that was very visual, that audiences of all ages could enjoy and that got them involved. Ballroom dancing has always been wonderful to watch; the old *Come Dancing* television show was great in its day. *Strictly Come Dancing*, however, not only has the dancing, the glamour, the music and the competition but also the celebrities and the reality-TV content. I'm not a fan of reality-TV; however, somehow it works in *Strictly Come Dancing*. The footage from the rehearsal studio lets audiences in on the effort that goes into dancing; if you didn't see how hard it is, there wouldn't be much point in watching it!

BRUCE FORSYTH

What sets *Strictly Come Dancing* aside from other celebrity reality shows is that our contestants aren't just there to raise their profiles – they're there to learn a completely new skill, and they have to work hard to stay on the show. The level of training that they had to do took everyone by surprise: originally, they were contracted to do just a few hours a week, but they ended up doing over six hours a day. The dedication was extraordinary: the dancers followed the celebrities all over the country to fit the training in, and Esther Rantzen even flew Anton du Beke out to join her on a cruise. That degree of dedication comes across on the Saturday night, and it gets everyone involved.

Mind you, it has provided a boost to a lot of careers, and in that respect *Strictly Come Dancing* has turned out to be a shot in the arm for television entertainment in general. Look at Julian Clary – he's doing the lottery show now, Jill Halfpenny is dancing in *Chicago* and, of course, Natasha never looked back.

We've spent a lot of time discussing exactly what it is that makes *Strictly Come Dancing* so successful – is it the competitive element, or the celebrities, or the judging, or the voting? But I think in the end what makes it work is that it's an aspirational show. The viewers get a chance to see people doing something very well indeed, and they watch them learning and training and think that's something they might do themselves. It's a live show, it's exciting and glamorous, and all the family can watch it together – that's a rare thing on television nowadays.

TESS DALY

History of the Show

Everyone remembers the television series Come Dancing – *those stiff, smiling mannequins gliding round the ballroom floor in yards of tulle and black penguin suits, the Rumbas, the Cha Cha Chas, the wonderful provincial Britishness of it all. But when the axe finally fell on* Come Dancing *in 1995 after years of dwindling audiences, it would have been a brave soul indeed who could have predicted that, less than a decade later, the format would have been made over into the biggest entertainment hit on British television in years.*

'It was one of those ideas that came about quite unexpectedly,' says Karen Smith, executive producer of *Strictly Come Dancing*. 'They were all sitting round in a commissioning meeting at BBC1, talking about celebrity programmes and new formats, and Fenia Vardanis, entertainment commissioning executive, said, "Why don't we bring back *Come Dancing* – but with celebs?" Everyone laughed at first, but the more they thought about it the more they liked it – and that's when I was brought in.'

Smith came from a solid background in light-entertainment events – she'd produced *Comic Relief does Fame Academy* for the BBC and *The Games*, a celebrity-athletics contest, for Channel 4. 'I knew absolutely nothing about the dance world,' she says, 'but that didn't seem to matter. What I did know about was doing big live-TV events with a competition element. The rest I could learn.'

That was in autumn 2003 – which gave Smith and her team only 24 weeks in which to put the show together from scratch. There was no format and no team – just a conviction that the combination of old-fashioned dancing and new-style celebrity

competition would work. 'I had faith in the idea from the beginning,' says Smith, 'because it seemed to appeal to such a wide range of people. We knew we were aiming for the Saturday-evening slot, the Holy Grail of scheduling, and the potential audience is enormous. Everyone from eight to 80 is available in theory, so if a show's going to work in that slot it has to appeal right across the board. I knew that the celebrity aspect would get the 20- and 30-something audience hooked. The music and dancing would appeal to the older audiences. And then there were the spangly frocks, the Barbie Doll quality that would bring in the little girls.'

Confident that *Pro-Celebrity Come Dancing*, as it was then called, worked in theory, Smith set about devising a format that would combine the competitive edge of *Pop Idol* and the breathtaking skill of the professional dance world. She contacted dancers and judges, she went to competitions around the country and immersed herself in the strange new world of ballroom and Latin. She watched tapes of the old *Come Dancing* series to see what, if anything, could be salvaged from a seemingly outdated formula. And, crucially, she worked out a voting system that would

'*Why don't we bring back* Come Dancing – *but with celebs?*'

give equal weight to professional judges and viewing public. 'That's a difficult balancing act. If you give all the power to the viewers, like in *Pop Idol*, then there's going to be a landslide win for someone regardless of their dancing skills; they'll get votes because they're popular. If the pro judges have all the power, then the viewers have no input. That was the problem with *Come Dancing*; you just saw these one-dimensional figures, you knew nothing about them, there was no reason to feel involved. The dancers just seemed like bizarre comedy people; you didn't see behind the façade. By working out a voting system that gives equal weight to the judges and the viewers, we ensure that the contestants are marked for their dancing ability and for their personality. That's the key to the show's

Over the 50s and 60s, Come Dancing *was the darling of British light entertainment and drew in huge audiences on a regular basis. Eventually though the times caught up with it and the dated-looking programme was axed in 1995.*

success. It doesn't alienate the serious dance fans, and it draws in that big Saturday-night audience.'

The next step was casting the professional dancers. There were eight in the first series, four men and four women – and they had to be the best in the business in order to give *Strictly Come Dancing* the credibility it would need to attract celebrity contestants. 'I had no idea at first just how famous these people were,' says Smith. 'They could be the

Stepping out: Tess Daly and Bruce Forsyth head up the dancers and celebrities involved in the first series.

world champion, but they could walk down the street in Britain and no one would know them. They're incredibly famous in Japan and America, where ballroom dancing is taken very seriously – but here they're only known by the real hardcore. Most of them live in flats and semis in south-east London, because that's where the best teachers are – but in Japan they're mobbed by huge screaming crowds. When Donnie Burns, the 14-times world Latin champion, visited Japan recently, he outsold Prince at the Tokyo Dome!'

With her format and her dancers in place, Smith, Richard Hopkins (Head of Format Entertainment)

and the Format Entertainment Development team set about selling the project to BBC1, BBC3 and BBC Worldwide, who would be screening or selling the show all over the world. 'We knew it was a winner, but we knew it was going to be a hard sell, so we made a point of turning up at all the pitching meetings with a couple of dancers in tow. We'd outline the format, so they could see it was rock solid, then we'd unleash the dancers. As soon as you see them in action, it's breathtaking. It clinched it every time.'

*'I knew we had to have someone
for everyone. I really wanted
Christopher Parker, because he was in a
famous soap, the young girls love him'*

And then came the really hard part: casting the celebrities. They had to be famous; there's no point in putting on a Saturday-night celebrity show with a bunch of people nobody's heard of. They had to commit themselves to 13 weeks of hard physical work for an untried format that looked, on paper, like a bizarre collision of the kitsch and the *passé*. Smith drew up a shortlist and set about wooing them.

'I knew we had to have someone for everyone. I really wanted Christopher Parker, because he was in a famous soap, the young girls love him and so do the mums and grandmas. Martin Offiah is a big tough rugby player, and he made it ok for men to watch.

Putting on the Ritz: a newly suave Christopher Parker prepares to brush the dust of Walford from his shoes.

Claire Sweeney has that girl-next-door thing. Lesley Garrett brought in an older, more highbrow audience. And David Dickinson ticks every single box; he even gets the student. It sounds quite calculated, but you have to be.'

Some of the people Smith approached were up for the job straight away; others took more persuading. 'I wanted Natasha Kaplinsky right from the start, because of that great tradition of news readers like Angela Rippon stepping out from behind the desk and

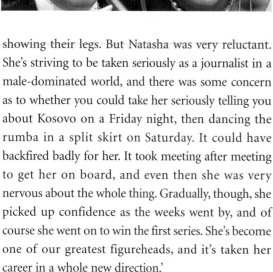

showing their legs. But Natasha was very reluctant. She's striving to be taken seriously as a journalist in a male-dominated world, and there was some concern as to whether you could take her seriously telling you about Kosovo on a Friday night, then dancing the rumba in a split skirt on Saturday. It could have backfired badly for her. It took meeting after meeting to get her on board, and even then she was very nervous about the whole thing. Gradually, though, she picked up confidence as the weeks went by, and of course she went on to win the first series. She's become one of our greatest figureheads, and it's taken her career in a whole new direction.'

Casting the second series was a whole lot easier; after viewing figures of 9.6 million for the final, celebrities were queueing up at Smith's door. 'We finished on Saturday, 3 July, and I went on holiday on the Monday. Then I got a call on the Tuesday asking if BBC1 could have another series in mid-October, running up to Christmas. I hadn't expected it to run till after Christmas – this only gave me 16 weeks from one series finishing to the next one starting. We had to find a couple of new dancers,

plus ten new celebrities, new costumes, new music, a new production team… It was a hell of a risk. The viewing figures had been good for the first series – but people might have felt it was too much too soon. In the event, it came together fine, and people loved it – but it was real seat-of-the-pants stuff.'

The gamble paid off, and the second series became the BBC's biggest Saturday-night hit in years. 'It's become exactly what a Saturday-night show should be – it's a safe place where nothing bad will happen, a little piece of magic. You can sit down with your children or your grandmother, and you know it's going to be glamorous, glitzy, funny, dramatic, tense and thoroughly entertaining. The competition element means it never gets dull, the music and dancing and design make it gorgeous to look at, and the personalities draw you in. And it has to work on a more sophisticated level too; there has to be just the right element of tongue-in-cheek humour about it to put it across in the 21st century. I never wanted it to be camp or parodic, but there has to be a bit of good-natured irony. You can have a laugh about it, but you can enjoy it for what it is at the same time.'

History of Come Dancing

BBC television had only just been back in business after the War when it launched *Come Dancing* in October 1949. It was the brainchild of Eric Morley, a young, freshly demobbed impresario who had just got a job with dance promoters Mecca – and who, thanks to *Come Dancing* and *Miss World*, would become one of the most powerful men in British variety in the 60s and 70s. *Come Dancing* started off as a live broadcast from regional ballrooms around the country, where couples would compete while professional dancers Syd Perkins and Edna Duffield gave tips and teaching advice. The first show was from the Manchester Ritz Ballroom; within a year, it was an established hit, and soon dropped the educational slant to become a straightforward competition. In 1953, the long-lasting format of regional heats and a national final were introduced.

Morley was the show's original master of ceremonies, but he was eventually supplanted by a string of celebrity presenters – and over the years they included Terry Wogan, Angela Rippon, Judith Chalmers, Keith Fordyce, Rosemarie Ford, Brian Johnston, Michael Aspel, David Jacobs and even Noel Edmonds.

Over the years, *Come Dancing* tried to keep up with the times, introducing rock 'n' roll dancing in the 50s, even disco in the 70s – but in the end it seemed terminally old-fashioned. It was moved to later and later slots, audiences declined, and it was finally axed in 1995.

International Versions

The success of *Strictly Come Dancing* sparked an extraordinary scramble for foreign rights to the show, and now audiences around the world have become immersed in the finer points of ballroom dancing. 'It's taken me completely by surprise,' says *SCD* executive producer Karen Smith. 'The format has sold all over Europe, in America and Australia, and we're currently talking to Japan. The only problem there is that they want to gunge the losers, which isn''t really in the spirit of the thing.'

The American version, *Dancing with the Stars*, played to enormous audiences on ABC, and was their biggest entertainment show for years. Boxer Evander Holyfield competed, but was beaten by *General Hospital* star Kelly Monaco. In Australia, the show was such a success that Channel Seven ran two series back to back.

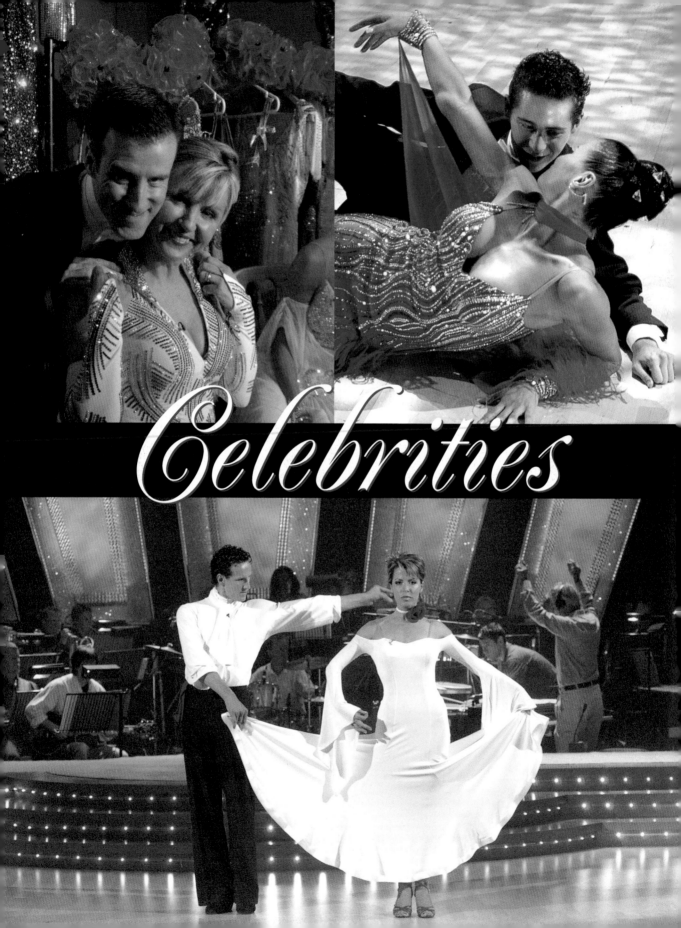

Celebrities

Series One

David Dickinson

He knows his way around a piece of antique mahogany, but could bargain-king David Dickinson cut it on the dance floor? And how far would his cult following take him when the competition got tough?

NAME David Dickinson
DAY JOB TV presenter, antiques expert
DANCE PARTNER Camilla Dallerup
BEST DANCE The Quickstep in week two, to 'Let's Face the Music and Dance'. 'You took off!' said Bruno, not the hardest man to please.
WORST DANCE The Cha Cha Cha in week one. Despite an impressive sparkly outfit, Dickinson looked ill at ease and unfit, and only scored 16.
THE JUDGES SAID Len: 'You're a marvellous sport, but you're too nice a guy for the Tango.'
HOW DID THEY DO? Knocked out after three weeks.

As the senior contestant in the first series, David Dickinson was brought into the mix to appeal to older viewers – but, as canny executive producer Karen Smith was well aware, his audience stretched right through to students and children, thanks to his catchphrase-heavy performance on *Bargain Hunt*. During the training there was much speculation as to whether he would prove to be a 'bobby-dazzler' or simply 'cheap as chips', but the laughs started to wear off when he threw himself into training with Camilla Dallerup. It soon became clear that Dickinson, for all his worldly charm, wasn't a dance natural; in fact, he seemed almost entirely lacking a sense of rhythm.

Then the Dickinson–Dallerup dance-floor début made an unforgettable impact. Bruce Forsyth had given him a big build-up as they'd chosen the song 'Sex Bomb' for their inaugural Cha Cha Cha. While Dallerup tried to hold the judges' eyes, Dickinson walked around the floor waggling his hands and visibly counting the beats. The judges were less than impressed. 'It's all pomp and no circumstance,' said Arlene Phillips, to which Dickinson offered a tart rejoinder: 'At 62, I try my best, love.' He clearly wasn't pleased with the harsh verdict, but returned after a week of intensive training to execute a creditable quickstep. The scores reflected the improvement, but it wasn't enough to save them, and Dickinson was knocked out in the third week.

Lesley Garrett

If they awarded points for enthusiasm, Lesley Garrett would have won the first series hands down. No other dancer threw herself into the show with such gusto, or enjoyed it so much – but that wasn't always enough to impress the judges.

Public performance held no fear for Lesley Garrett, whose operatic career has taken her to audiences all over the world. But dancing isn't quite the same, as she was the first to admit. Partner Anton du Beke provided the necessary inspiration, and as the training progressed Garrett found her wings. 'No matter how hectic my day is, I come here and my spirit soars,' she said, and didn't even complain when du Beke fell, hard, on top of her during rehearsal.

Garrett's dance-floor début surprised even her. In a figure-hugging mauve dress, with her hair up, she glided through a Waltz to 'He was Beautiful', and she was so excited when she completed a successful first round that she let out an ear-splitting soprano shriek. 'That was the most exciting moment of my whole life,' she told Tess Daly backstage, visibly shaking to prove it. They ended the first show with the best scores from the judges and looked like favourites to win.

As the weeks went on, the pounds fell off; Garrett had to attend constant costume refittings as her body shape changed. Her dancing improved too, and in the third week she and du Beke fought heavy colds to deliver a very respectable Rumba. Their scores kept high, audiences liked them, but cracks began to appear in the sixth week when she admitted she was 'tetchy and cross', finding it hard to learn the Foxtrot. The judges liked what she did and they worked hard but, in a controversial decision, they were knocked out in the seventh week when viewers saved Christopher Parker for the final. Garrett was in tears, but quickly rallied her spirits. 'I think every woman on the planet should have half an hour with Anton du Beke,' she enthused.

NAME Lesley Garrett, CBE

DAY JOB Opera singer

DANCE PARTNER Anton du Beke

BEST DANCE Best and worst came in the same week. The Foxtrot in week six earned 34 points, inspiring Bruno Tonioli to call her 'a class act'.

WORST DANCE Later in the same show, the Cha Cha Cha to Kylie Minogue's 'Spinning Around' let her down. She started off on the wrong foot, and never really recovered.

THE JUDGES SAID Arlene: 'You have a dancer inside of you, and I'd like to see it come out.'

HOW DID THEY DO? Third place, knocked out after the seventh show.

Verona Joseph

Strictly Come Dancing proved an uphill struggle for actor Verona Joseph, who was not only filming all day but trying to move house as well.

NAME Verona Joseph
DAY JOB Actor, plays Jess Griffin in *Holby City*
DANCE PARTNER Paul Killick
BEST DANCE Weirdly, Joseph got the best marks for the dance that broke the rules, the Cha Cha Cha in the first week.
WORST DANCE Their remaining three dances all scored a respectable 24, but marks could have been higher if they'd stayed within the rule book.
THE JUDGES SAID Bruno: 'Buckets of sex appeal.' Len: 'All sizzle, no sausage.'
HOW DID THEY DO? Knocked out after the fourth show.

It was never going to be easy for Verona Joseph, who fitted the programme and training into her commitment to BBC1's war-horse, *Holby City*. Dance partner Paul Killick travelled to and from the BBC's Elstree Studios to rehearse with Joseph in her breaks – but the pressure was showing from the start, with the actor complaining of fainting fits and panic attacks. You'd never have known it, however, when they stepped out in the first show, she in a green spangled dress, he in a leopardskin jacket, to deliver a controversial Cha Cha Cha. Killick ended the dance by lifting his partner off the floor and spinning her around – which got the judges in a fury. 'You broke a rule!' shrieked Arlene, but the duo were unrepentant.

It was clear from the start that Joseph was a dance natural – and there were even mutterings from other dancers that she was professionally trained and so had an unfair advantage. 'My professional training to date was three weeks of ballet when I was seven, and four weeks of contemporary dance when I was 14,' she said. 'If that means I'm a professional dancer, then my mum got value for money, darling!'

But stress was getting the better of Joseph by the fourth week – not only was Killick proving to be a hard taskmaster but she was also in the throes of moving house. Their Paso Doble was done on a wing and a prayer and minimum rehearsal, and despite the fact that both of them looked hotter than hell on the dance floor, their scores crashed, and they were knocked out. Joseph seemed relieved. 'Now I can concentrate on moving,' she said. 'Paul deserved someone who could give him 100 per cent.'

Martin Offiah

He excels on the rugby field – but could Martin 'Chariots' Offiah cut it on the dance floor?

There was no doubt that Martin Offiah was fit – apart from a niggling old shoulder injury he was in full match form. But there's a big difference between the strength and stamina required for rugby, and the grace and co-ordination demanded by ballroom dancing. 'I've danced a bit in nightclubs,' said Offiah, 'but nothing with the discipline of ballroom.' As he trained with Erin Boag, he soon realised that dance was not a soft option – but it had compensations. 'I'd rather dance with a woman in a skimpy outfit than play rugby with a load of sweaty geezers,' he said.

Offiah's first outing with Erin was a Waltz, and he surprised everyone by getting through it with some style. He was far from relaxed, though, and the tension was written all over his face. Len Goodman was encouraging, but Arlene Phillips gave a double-edged compliment: 'For a rugby player, you dance very well.'

However, his confidence boosted, Offiah soon relaxed and as the weeks progressed his dancing – and his dress sense – improved. Sober suits went out, and revealing outfits appeared in various hot shades. Offiah's Jive in the third week got a standing ovation – and not just because he'd overcome an ankle injury to perform it. The newspapers started to buzz with some half-hearted rumours that Offiah and Boag were clicking off the dance floor as well as on, but Offiah squashed that talk: 'Erin is like Alex Ferguson to me. She's the toughest manager I've ever had. I nearly had a dance shoe in the head.'

Sadly, Offiah fell victim to the Parker Factor. As Chris Parker's popularity soared in inverse proportion to his dancing ability, Offiah was knocked out.

NAME Martin Offiah MBE
DAY JOB Wigan and England rugby player
DANCE PARTNER Erin Boag
BEST DANCE Best first for Offiah: his Waltz in the first show scored 25 from the judges.
WORST DANCE The Rumba in show two only scored 21 ('No hip action,' complained Craig), as did the Jive the following week ('Glued to the floor,' said Arlene).
THE JUDGES SAID Craig: 'You put your butt to much better use!' Arlene: 'Charming, but lazy legs.'
HOW DID THEY DO? Knocked out after the sixth show.

Natasha Kaplinsky

Although the most reluctant of contestants, Natasha Kaplinsky discovered a hidden talent for dance and enjoyed the experience so much not only did she win – but also went on to co-present part of the next series.

Natasha Kaplinsky was not *Strictly Come Dancing*'s most eager recruit. 'I begged my bosses to ban me from doing the show,' she says. 'I'd worked so hard to build up my credibility as a newsreader, as a woman in a male-dominated world, and I thought this could throw it all away. At one point I was seriously considering "falling" off the kerb and twisting my ankle. But it didn't work, and I ended up in training.'

Kaplinsky's is the most dramatic of all the transformations wrought by the show. Within weeks, she'd discovered a new confidence and dance ability that she never knew she had. 'It was by far the most frightening thing I've done in my life. I've presented some pretty big news stories, but nothing can compare with the terror of going out in front of millions of people on live television to do something that I didn't think I could do. The producers tried to win me round by showing me some dresses, but I saw them, imagined revealing myself in that way, and I just shrank into a corner. But once I got dancing, and realized I could do it, my attitude changed. I'd only had two dance lessons in my life, when I was about six – but suddenly I was acquiring a new skill. Brendan [Cole] was a real perfectionist, but he knew when not to push me. Sometimes I was so close to the edge I would have just walked out, but when I was feeling strong, he was ruthless. It was as much about emotional coaching as physical training. The sense of achievement is like nothing else I've ever experienced.'

Kaplinsky was overwhelmed by the support of the voting public; but she also found herself splashed all over the newspapers. 'I've been a journalist all my working life, but I was shocked at the extent to which the papers started to write about me and the other contestants. It was pretty horrible, and I couldn't bear to think that people might believe the things that were being made up about me – but, to be honest, I was getting up at 3am, doing breakfast news, then rehearsing all day for Saturday; there wasn't time to get upset.' The experience, although traumatic, was very positive for Kaplinsky – so she returned to co-present the first part of series two with Bruce Forsyth.

NAME Natasha Kaplinsky

DAY JOB Presents BBC1's *Breakfast News*

DANCE PARTNER Brendan Cole

BEST DANCE Natasha and Brendan pulled out all the stops for the Samba in week five, and scored 37 – possibly inspired by the presence of Brendan's mother, visiting from New Zealand!

WORST DANCE Only 24 out of 40 for the week-three Jive, marked down for breaking the rules.

THE JUDGES SAID Arlene: 'Staggering! You are a professional dancer!' Len: 'If they don't win, it's a travesty.'

HOW DID THEY DO? Winner of series one; Kaplinsky liked it so much she co-presented part of series two!

Christopher Parker

The EastEnders *pin-up proved that you don't have to be a great dancer to get the public vote – but would Christopher Parker be able to cope with the weekly grilling he got from the judges?*

It didn't start well. Christopher Parker, idol of millions of teenage girls for his puppy-dog performance as Albert Square's Spencer Moon, was the first to admit that he had 'two left feet'. Even his *EastEnders* co-star Shane Richie urged him to 'Please walk away! You can't even walk in time!' Parker laughed off the criticism at first and threw himself into training with his partner, Hanna Karttunen, but it was apparent from the very first show that he was hampered by an almost total absence of aptitude. The pair's Cha Cha Cha, to 'Lady Marmalade', featured some fancy footwork from Karttunen, but not much from Parker.

The public took to Parker, and brought him back week after week ('He's like a boomerang!' said Bruce Forsyth), but the judges were a different matter, and soon their regular humiliation of Parker became one of the show's must-see moments. Parker didn't take it lying down. By the sixth week, he was fighting back. After a disastrous Paso Doble ('Paso dreadful, my darling!' wailed Bruno), which scored only 15 out of a possible 40, Parker was visibly upset. 'What do I have to do?' he pleaded. 'I'm trying my hardest!' Over the coming weeks his obvious, valiant efforts in rehearsal (not to mention his cute expressions of vulnerability and dismay) won the public's heart; Shane Richie started turning up to support his screen brother, and Parker made it into the final. But the judges were implacable, basing their scores not on Parker's lovable personality but on his dancing. Everyone hated them for it, and Parker crashed out of a final he never expected to reach.

NAME Christopher Parker

DAY JOB Actor, best known as Spencer Moon in *EastEnders*

DANCE PARTNER Hanna Karttunen

BEST DANCE The Foxtrot in week four. Christopher and Hanna glided around the floor to Westlife's 'Flying without Wings', and ended the dance in a romantic clinch.

THE JUDGES were kind. 'Even Arlene was positive!' gasped a shocked Parker.

WORST DANCE The samba in week five, and the Paso Doble in week six, which prompted Bruno Tonioli to say 'You were stamping on cockroaches!'

THE JUDGES SAID 'If there were an award for bravery,' said Arlene, in a rather backhanded compliment, 'you'd win it.' Craig was less charitable, and repeatedly called Christopher 'naff'.

STICKY MOMENTS In their first dance, Parker tripped over and got headbutted by Karttunen.

HOW DID THEY DO? Runners-up of series one.

Claire Sweeney

Expectations were high when Claire Sweeney, star of stage musicals, hit the Strictly Come Dancing *studio. But would it go her way or would the judges mark her too hard?*

NAME Claire Sweeney
DAY JOB Actor and TV presenter who also starred in the West End production of *Chicago*
DANCE PARTNER John Byrnes
BEST DANCE The Tango in week three. Len described her as 'a panther stalking its prey'.
WORST DANCE The Rumba in week two, which still managed to score a respectable 26. Len accused them of hiding the steps under flashy effects.
THE JUDGES SAID Bruno dismissed their début Waltz as 'boring,' but after their Paso Doble he described Claire as 'quite the sexiest bull I've seen.'
HOW DID THEY DO? Knocked out in week five.

'I'm not a good dancer,' insisted Claire Sweeney during training, 'I'm just someone who can get away with it.' But anyone who had seen her gliding through the Waltz with professional partner John Byrnes would have found that hard to believe – and Sweeney had to battle with her enhanced reputation for the rest of the show. When the judges marked her harshly, Sweeney complained, 'I can only do my best! I'm not a trained dancer!' and she never really recovered from that initial disappointment.

That's not to say that she didn't give the show her best shot. In fact, Sweeney and Byrnes stayed high in the ranking throughout their five weeks on the show, but in the end they failed to win enough public sympathy to keep them in the competition. In the third week, their fiery Tango inspired the judges to get out their '9' paddles for the first time in the competition, and they ended the show at the top of the table, well ahead of their nearest rivals, Lesley and Anton.

But, at the end of week five, the viewers decided to vote them off. 'I feel disappointed, obviously,' said Sweeney after the shock result came through. 'I really enjoyed tonight; it was the first time it didn't feel like a competition. Maybe I was having too much fun.' She'd realised – too late in the event – that the key to *Strictly Come Dancing* success wasn't just fancy footwork, but audience sympathy. 'We had a plan if we got through this week,' she said. 'I was going to get myself photographed with a plaster cast on one of my legs.'

Jason Wood

Unknown to prime-time audiences, would Jason Wood prove to be the unexpected hit of the series? Only if he could learn to dance well enough to impress the judges…

It seemed like a marriage made in heaven: Jason Wood, the critically lauded stand-up comedian, and world dance champion Kylie Jones. Kylie and Jason; it had worked before, so why not for *Strictly Come Dancing*? But it soon became clear that Wood wasn't working, either for the judges or the audiences. He seemed nervous from the start, unsure whether to send up the whole thing as a camp joke, or to knuckle down and concentrate on the dancing. It didn't help that there was over 12 inches difference in their heights; 'It's like Beauty and the Beast,' said Wood during training. 'Maybe being so abnormal we might just win some hearts.'

They took to the studio floor in the first week with a Waltz – the most elegant of dances – but Wood couldn't stop playing it for laughs, constantly pulling faces and rolling his eyes. Arlene Phillips picked up on it straight away: 'Jason was waltzing with his face more than he was with his feet,' she said. Wood was clearly stung, and realised he had to rely on choreography rather than comedy. By week two's Rumba, he was in much better shape. 'Last week it was like dragging round a jumbo jet,' he said, 'this week I was a little cruiser', and Len Goodman agreed: 'From a caterpillar to a butterfly!' Even Phillips was converted, calling Wood's performance 'sensual' (which prompted some wag in the audience to yell out, 'Put your glasses on!').

But they still didn't score highly, and the audience vote wasn't enough to save them. 'Nobody wants to go out first,' said Wood, 'but I have to say I've enjoyed every minute. Dancing with Kylie was like having a little bit of magic in my arms.'

NAME Jason Wood
DAY JOB Stand-up comedian and musical impressionist
DANCE PARTNER Kylie Jones
BEST DANCE Their first-week Waltz to 'Three Times a Lady', which gained 21 points.
WORST DANCE Their Rumba in week two impressed some judges, but prompted Craig Revel Horwood to award a stingy two points.
THE JUDGES SAID Craig: 'Jason was cheesy, lumpy and awkward. He should take this competition a little more seriously.'
HOW DID THEY DO? First to leave series one, in the third week.

A Few Moments from *Series One*

Production and Location

The gorgeous dance hall that we see every week on Strictly Come Dancing *looks like everyone's fantasy of the perfect nightclub: a huge floor accessed by a sweeping staircase, a glamorous bandstand, lights, curtains, arches and an audience seated at tables and chairs. But it's all an illusion; it's actually a set that comes to pieces after every show and is stashed away in a corner of BBC Television Centre in west London.*

The lights return to the warehouse, the curtains are folded, the chairs stacked. Even the dance floor breaks up into dozens of pieces, waiting for the following week when the whole thing is slowly, laboriously and painstakingly reassembled, and the illusion begins all over again.

The first question that everyone asks is, 'Why?' Wouldn't it just be easier to build a semi-permanent set that lasts for the duration of the series, thus avoiding the time, labour and expense of striking, storing and rebuilding it after every show? The answer, incredibly, is that it's actually easier and cheaper to do it this way. Studio One at Television Centre (universally known as TC1) is the best-equipped studio in the country, and *Strictly Come Dancing* – a live-music and performance show with complex lights and a real-time voting component – demands all the resources that the modern TV producer has at their disposal. Of course, it would be impossible to book TC1 for the entire eight-week run as it's also home to a lot of other regular BBC shows, including *Blue Peter* and *Top of the Pops*, plus occasional specials like *Children in Need* and S*ports Personality of the Year*. To run the show from a smaller, less well-equipped studio would bring its own headaches – not least

necessitating a far greater reliance on hired equipment, which is extremely expensive. The first series of *Strictly Come Dancing* came from the smaller TC4, and when the second series was commissioned the decision was taken to move the show to the larger, state-of-the-art studio space, from which there's been no turning back.

'There are cheaper spaces available,' says studio resources manager Simon Littler, whose job it is to oversee every aspect of the physical production of the weekly show, 'but they can work out to be a lot more expensive. You'd have to go outside the M25 to a studio like Pinewood or Shepperton – and then you'd have to hire lights for the entire duration of the run, you'd have to transport everyone to and from the studio, pay for accommodation and build all the travelling time into the schedule. It's just not worth it. If we're in TC1 everyone can get there easily, we only have to hire lights for three days a week, and we have everything we need right there.'

STRICTLY ON SCHEDULE

Working within this extraordinarily tight framework, the *Strictly Come Dancing* team has evolved a weekly timetable that sounds almost impossible to maintain, yet which has kept the show running without major

headaches for two series. In order to be ready for the live show on Saturday, they need to get into TC1 on Wednesday, as soon as the previous show moves out. The studio is basically a lightproof, soundproof box with a very flat floor, 10,500 square feet in size, and everything that you see on screen has to be put there deliberately. The first thing to go in is lighting, and

Saturday night, and the Strictly Come Dancing *set is reassembled, dressed, lit and ready for another show.*

Littler's team would start rigging overnight on Wednesday, into Thursday morning. There are 300 lighting hoists in TC1, including a lot of 'specials' – lights that move, project patterns or follow the dancers, which are programmed and remote-controlled from the director's gallery – all of which have to be installed and wired up before anything else can be done. Some of the lights live in Television Centre, but several have to be hired in specially, and they arrive on 40-foot trucks, which have to be unloaded into the studio in the small hours of Thursday morning.

By 6am on Thursday all the lighting should be in place, every light plugged into the control board and ready to be programmed by the lighting designer. That's when the scenic team take over and start building (or, rather, rebuilding) the familiar dance palace that forms the set of *Strictly Come Dancing*. They start off with the large mezzanine area behind the drapes and the stairs – from where we see the presenters appearing at the beginning of every show, and where the dancers are interviewed after their performances. The rest of the set is built around that: the stairs, the bandstand, the dance floor and the judges' area. Some of the pieces, such as the sweeping staircase, are very big and can simply be wheeled into TC1 and bolted on to the mezzanine. Others, such as the flying arches, are smaller and more fiddly, and have to be more or less rebuilt after every show.

The most complicated piece of the set is also the most important: the dance floor. Specially designed by *Strictly Come Dancing*'s set designer Patrick Doherty, it consists of a metal framework that sits on a layer of foam on the studio's concrete floor (which has to be freshly painted every week), topped off with a cladding of plywood and a parquet surface. It has to be bouncy enough to give the dancers' legs the kind of shock absorption that they need, but it also has to be thin and light enough to be transported and stored in between shows. The secret of the *Strictly Come Dancing* floor is that it comes to pieces – about 20 individual bits (large enough that they can be comfortably carried by two men) that are brought into the studio and put together like a giant jigsaw for every show.

Once the floor is in place, the audience areas are built on decking that sits on the studio floor, and then, while the carpenters and painters are putting the finishing touches to the joins and edges of the set, the electricians arrive to install the hundreds of little colour-changing LEDs that deck the staircase and arches. 'We've made a time-lapse film of the set being put together,' says Simon Littler, 'and it's amazing to watch. There are hundreds of people involved every single time we do it; it's slow and labour-intensive but it works.'

By Friday afternoon, all the hard work has paid off, and the studio is ready for the first camera rehearsal. 'That's the deadline that we're all aiming for. In theory, every tablecloth is in place, every bit of carpet nailed down before the cameras start working. It sounds impossible, but we've had plenty of practice now, so generally speaking it's all there on time.'

The camera rehearsal involves the dancers going through their paces on the floor, making sure that everything's ready for the live show on Saturday. 'Everything has to be in place,' says Littler, 'because it's live television. If something goes wrong, you can't go for a retake. We have to have systems in place that cover every eventuality – that's why it's such a long set-up. People sometimes ask me why I have such a big team of

Blackpool

At least once during series one and two, *Strictly Come Dancing* decamped for a live show to the Tower Ballroom, Blackpool – the spiritual home of ballroom dancing. 'We usually had to go because there was a big event pre-booked into TC1,' says Littler, 'but it became a great tradition on the show. The challenges at Blackpool are very different. Obviously we had a ready-made set, and it's the most wonderful interior – but it's not fitted up for live

broadcasts at all. We had to run miles of cables into the

theatre from a generator, going through the doors and windows and over the theatre balcony. Then we had to build cages to protect all the outside-broadcast equipment; Blackpool is a pretty lively place on a Saturday night, and if we hadn't fenced all our stuff into a pound it would have just got destroyed. We even had to get police and local-authority permission to remove benches from the pedestrian area outside the theatre so that we could park our trucks. It was a huge operation, and those were very, very late nights.'

'*While the programme is on air, most of the behind-the-scenes team are sittng up in the gallery, making sure that everything is going according to plan.*'

people in the studio who don't seem to be doing very much a lot of the time. The truth is that for every bit of kit that could possibly go wrong you have to have someone keeping an eye out. It's a bit like building a house of cards in a hurricane: it only works if you have one person to hold every single card in place.'

THE SHOW GOES ON

After all the preparation, the *Strictly Come Dancing* set is only in place for a few hours. The band comes in on Saturday morning for its soundcheck, the presenters and dancers come out of make-up and then, on

As you'll never see it: technical operations carry on right up until the last moment before the show starts.

Saturday afternoon, everyone is ready for the dress rehearsal. After that, the audience is allowed into the studio, and the show is on.

While the programme is on air, most of the behind-the-scenes team are sitting up in the gallery, making sure that everything is going according to plan. Littler's job is to keep an eye on everything that's going on – fire-fighting problems as they turn up and, crucially, making sure that the live feed is

Production facts

The total number of hours danced by the couples, in training and performance, is 934: that's 38.9 days, or 5.5 weeks, or 1.38 months

A dancer can cover around five miles of ground in a six-hour evening, which means that *Strictly Come Dancing*'s couples have covered 778 miles in the course of their training

The total number of telephone votes cast so far is 1,251,579

The total amount of money raised for Children in Need and Comic Relief is £1,520,184,18

being picked up by both BBC1 and BBC3. 'If the feed does go down,' Littler says, 'There's a reserve in place, and that's my call. We can never allow ourselves to risk just having blank screens.'

But it's not all high-tech. 'We actually spend a lot of time in the gallery adding up the judges' scores in our heads. We could have given them fancy voting equipment that added up the scores automatically, but Karen [Smith, the executive producer] decided from the word go that the judges really had to have paddles with numbers on that they would hold up. The floor manager sneaks in to see the judges a few seconds before they announce their scores, they tell him what they're going to award, and he jumps out of shot to radio the scores up to Karen and me. So we stand around going, "Eight… six… that's 14… plus six is 20, plus seven… 27! 27!", checking each other's mental arithmetic.'

Fortunately, the rest of the voting is taken care of by a much more sophisticated electronic system that logs all the viewers' calls in time for the results show later on Saturday evening. 'And once that's in, my only remaining job is to make sure that everyone who needs a taxi has got one.'

The Dancers

The professional dancers have the hardest job on Strictly Come Dancing. *They're not just responsible for getting onto the studio floor week in, week out, performing effortlessly elegant, exciting dances and putting up with the sometimes unkind remarks of the judges, but they also have to train celebrities who, let's face it, may not have a natural aptitude for dancing.*

They also have to choose music for each dance, create choreography to make the most of their partner's ability, and co-ordinate costume and make-up into a single entity that will, hopefully, get them through to the following week's show.

'We're pretty competitive,' says Anton du Beke, now dancing into a third series of the show. 'We have to be, because in the professional dance world you won't get anywhere without a competitive streak. So we're very committed to practising, just like any athlete, and we have to be on top of every aspect of the performance. When we signed up to do the first series, we were only contracted to rehearse for six hours a week. It ended up being six hours a day, or more. We had to fit around the celebrities' lives; in my case that meant following Lesley Garrett on her tour all over the country, fitting in rehearsals when we could. We all realized that we had to put the hours in, otherwise we'd have nothing to make a show out of come Saturday.'

The dancers are dedicated – but what about the celebrities? 'You can tell straight away if you've got something decent to work with,' says Darren Bennett, who partnered Jill Halfpenny to victory in the second series. 'Jill and I first met in a photographic studio, and as she took my hand I could feel her body weight – which means that she's conscious of where her body is in space. I asked her to extend a foot, and she did it instantly. I knew then that we had the potential to go all the way in the show, because she had innate ability. If someone can feel rhythm, count beats, and knows where their limbs are in relation to each other, you can teach them to dance. If they can't do those things, there's not a lot you can do. You can coach them to repeat sequences of steps, but they'll never dance. We see that all the time as teachers, and I think the viewers can see it on screen. Some of the celebrities literally could not hear rhythm. And we can't teach that. You've either got it or you haven't.'

Rehearsing became the most intense part of the *Strictly Come Dancing* experience for many of the professionals. 'We start five weeks before the first show,' says du Beke, 'and we develop a close relationship very quickly. You have to. Dance is very physical, and these people are learning from scratch, so they have to be able to take criticism. My job as a teacher is to give criticism without destroying the ego, and to send them out there feeling like a million dollars. That wasn't difficult with Lesley because she loved to dance and had natural ability. It was harder with Esther [Rantzen, in series two] because she had so much to learn. Esther is a woman and a half, but steps sort of elude her. I realised that she was going to be stepping out on to the studio floor, dressed in a revealing frock, dancing a Samba and being judged against someone like Sarah Manners, who looks like a supermodel. I had to give her the confidence to go out there feeling equal, with her own sexuality, her own charisma, that people would respond to. She underwent a metamorphosis that was extraordinary for a 64-year-old woman.'

'As dancers, we were all committed to making the show look as good as possible,' says Darren Bennett. 'I was staying up all night to get the choreography finished in time. Arlene Phillips once complimented me on a piece of choreography; little did she know that I'd sketched it out in my front room the night before, dancing round the furniture. The deadlines can get very hairy, and that's when your relationship with your celebrity really matters. If they can't take criticism, you're sunk. Luckily for me, Jill and I spoke our minds and swore at each other, and we didn't care. Because she's an actor, she understands that you have to get it right. None of us wanted to be involved in anything that would make ballroom look kitsch or silly. We get enough of that prejudice, and this was a chance to set the record straight.'

While everyone realised that *Strictly Come Dancing* could do just that, there was uncertainty right until the show was on air. 'It was a leap of faith,' says Anton du Beke, 'Live, ballroom dancing is wonderful and exciting – you've got gorgeous men and women, great dresses and incredible athleticism – but it can look cheesy on television, as we know from *Come Dancing*. It was important that people understood just how hard it is, like any sport. There was a moment in the first series when we all started taking it very seriously – it was, I think, the defining moment for the show. It was the first time anyone had been knocked out. We'd all been working so hard to get it on, we didn't think about results, and then we lost Jason [Wood] and Kylie [Jones]. There were a lot of tears – partly of relief, but also of sadness, because we realised that we might be next. That's when everyone dug in, and the show really took flight.'

Erin Boag

She's the epitome of grace and effortless style in her professional dancing life. But how would Erin Boag, the queen of ballroom, cope with a rugby player and a comedian leading her around the floor?

Erin Boag is a very determined woman. At the age of three, she persuaded her mother to take her to dance classes, and quickly mastered ballet, tap, jazz, ballroom and Latin. In her teens, she moved from her native New Zealand to Australia. When she moved to London she announced to her then-partner that she would be dancing in the International Dance Championships within a year and, although he laughed, 12 months later she was there. It sounds easy, but it was anything but. Boag split with her partner, and found herself alone in a foreign city. 'That was tough. I took four jobs to support myself; money was scarce. I remember sitting on a bus with my last pound, not knowing whether to laugh or cry.'

Then destiny, in the shape of Anton du Beke, came along, and they formed a partnership that took them to the top of the ballroom world. They turned professional in 2002; in 2003 they became the IDTA Classic Champions. But, as *Strictly Come Dancing* proves again and again, professional success in any sphere is no guarantee of victory in the studio.

In series one, Boag was paired with Martin Offiah: could she turn a hulking rugby player into a graceful ballroom butterfly? Amazingly, the answer seemed to be 'yes'. Offiah repeatedly paid tribute to Boag's training expertise, as he was transformed from a stiff, frightened-looking dummy into a graceful dancer. But, despite her best efforts, Boag was out of the show in the sixth week. She then demonstrated her loyalty to her professional partner by walking out wearing an 'Anton and Lesley' T-shirt.

In series two, Boag had a different challenge with Julian Clary. Again, Clary wasn't too comfortable in the ballroom, but Boag put him at ease, and their sense of fun soon shone through. By the middle of the series, Clary had improved, and even his arch-enemy, Craig Revel Horwood was forced to admit it. 'Erin's such a good teacher,' raved Clary. 'She's so persistently positive, and I absorb her confidence.' It was that confidence that took them to the final. In series three Erin is once more partnered by a top athlete; so will it be gold for her and Colin Jackson?

Darren Bennett

As one half of the winning team of the second series, Darren Bennett added one more trophy to an already enormous collection. With his dance partner (and wife) Lilia Kopylova he's won the International and British Youth Championships and, immediately after turning professional in 2003, they won the British Rising Star Professional Championships at their first attempt. Within a year they were ranking sixth in the world series.

Sheffield-born Bennett has been dancing since the age of six – which didn't come as much surprise to his parents, both of whom were professional dancers. He'd done so well as a junior that he had his first taste of TV fame in the mid-90s, appearing on the original *Come Dancing* show. His twin brother, Dale (yet another dancer in the Bennett family), introduced him to Kopylova. Their professional relationship blossomed and they decided to specialise in Latin, and their personal relationship didn't do badly either: they were married within 18 months.

Bennett was fortunate in his partner for *Strictly Come Dancing* – although, during the weeks leading up to the final, there were grumblings from some quarters that Jill Halfpenny was actually too good to be in the competition, having had some previous dance experience. Halfpenny was dismissive ('It's just a bit of gossip'), but Bennett was more philosophical. 'It's all about putting in a good performance every week so that they don't have a chance to give us a bad mark,' he said. And he wasn't wrong: they were the first couple ever to score a perfect 40 for their Jive to 'I'm Still Standing' in the final.

'Of course it was great to win, but the competition on the show isn't among the professional dancers. We have to get the celebrities do the best job they can. We help each other out with choreography and ideas. It's not our competition. We compete in a different arena.'

So the winner returns for series three. Can he defend his title with partner Gloria Hunniford?

John Byrnes

John Byrnes joined Strictly Come Dancing *as a consultant, adviser and go-between for the BBC in its negotiations with the professional dance world. 'There was a great concern among dancers, and dance organisations, that we should not be shown in a bad light. We live on our reputations; if they are damaged it can ruin our livelihood.*

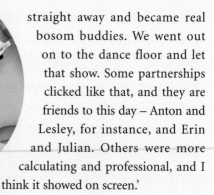

S o I needed a lot of assurance from the BBC that this wasn't going to be a mickey-take. We'd just emerged from that horrendous period when everyone thought ballroom dancing was tacky, all sequinned jumpsuits and huge collars, and we didn't want to do anything that was going to set us back.'

Byrnes advised executive producer Karen Smith on a range of technical points, from costuming to rehearsal time. He also introduced her to some dancers. 'I found myself in the unenviable position of representing the dance world to the BBC, and the BBC to the dance world. There were a lot of phone calls and emails going back and forth, and we were all very nervous. When we heard that they were going to call it *Strictly Come Dancing*, it started all over again; much as I love the film *Strictly Ballroom* (and I have a lot of friends who were in it), I didn't want to get involved in something that was aiming to get a cheap laugh out of ballroom dancing. We've all been dancing since we were kids, and we take it seriously.'

Eventually, the format was licked into shape to everyone's satisfaction – and Byrnes found himself partnering Claire Sweeney. 'Claire wanted to work hard and have fun. We hit it off

straight away and became real bosom buddies. We went out on to the dance floor and let that show. Some partnerships clicked like that, and they are friends to this day – Anton and Lesley, for instance, and Erin and Julian. Others were more calculating and professional, and I think it showed on screen.'

As the show launched the dance world still wondered whether it would be a curse or a blessing. 'There were people telling me that I'd made a big mistake, that I was going to drag dance down. After a few weeks, they changed their tune. They saw that the show was working, and that their businesses were flourishing as a result, and now everyone agrees that it was the best thing to happen to dance for years.'

Byrnes opted out of the second series; his wife, dancer Jane Lyttleton-Byrnes, had recently given birth to a son, and his dance school demanded more time than the show would allow. 'I was sorry not to be in the second series, but I'm still very satisfied at my part in the show. I've never been involved in anything on that level before, and even though I look back now and wonder how I managed, it was a tremendous experience.'

Nicole Cutler

Nicole Cutler didn't get much of a chance to show off her skills in the second series of Strictly Come Dancing. *Partnered with Diarmuid Gavin, she was soon out of the running – but not before she'd had a brave stab at turning the gardener into a dancer.*

'Diarmuid was never going to be a natural dancer,' she says, 'but he made up for it in other ways. He tried so hard, and he was very willing to learn – which is really all you can ask for as a teacher. I do a lot of professional teaching, and this experience really stretched me. Usually you're starting off with someone who has basic dance ability – a sense of rhythm, at least – otherwise they wouldn't be there. But Diarmuid just couldn't hear the rhythm at all. I had to think of new ways of explaining the dance to him, in terms that he would understand. In the end, I related all the choreography to gardening – I got him to think of the dance floor in terms of borders and lawns, with the steps as different plants, and so on. It was starting to work. In our final week, when we did the Paso Doble, he was starting to make real progress. It was frustrating that we were voted off the show that week, because I think we were heading for a breakthrough.'

Nicole Cutler has been dancing all her life: she started off in her native South Africa then scaled the heights of the professional Latin American circuit after she moved to the UK at the age of 18. For ten years she danced with her husband, Matthew (one of the professional dancers in the third series of *Strictly Come Dancing*), and together they became All England Professional Champions in 2004. Now she's partnered by Robin Sewell. 'Doing *Strictly Come Dancing* was a very useful experience for me,' she says. 'On a personal level, it's boosted my business: so many people want to learn how to dance, and to see professional dancers. But it's done a lot for the whole image of the business, too. People used to think we just ponced around in sequins, covered in fake tan. Now they can see how hard we work. Mind you, *Strictly Come Dancing* is ridiculously hard work. We're teaching a new dance in one week, from the start to performance; that's nearly impossible. We'd never have to do that in the real world.'

Camilla Dallerup

Danish dancing queen Camilla Dallerup found herself not just competing in a dance competition when she entered Strictly Come Dancing *but also starring in an unexpected soap opera.*

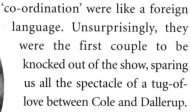

When her nine-year relationship with her personal and professional partner Brendan Cole came to an end during the show, the press was quick to point the finger at Natasha Kaplinsky as 'the other woman', and interest in all parties became intense. Sadly for Dallerup, most of her involvement with the show was destined to be off the dance floor, because she was unlucky in her choice of celebrity partner. While Cole waltzed away to victory with the multi-talented Ms Kaplinsky, Dallerup was saddled with David Dickinson, a man to whom the words 'rhythm' and 'co-ordination' were like a foreign language. Unsurprisingly, they were the first couple to be knocked out of the show, sparing us all the spectacle of a tug-of-love between Cole and Dallerup.

Dallerup has been dancing since the age of two, when her mother took her to her first dance classes at home in Aalborg, Denmark. She took to it like a duck to water, and by the age of six was sneaking into dance competitions that, technically, you had to be eight to enter. She won the Danish Junior Championships at the age of 12, and started visiting the UK to compete. She met Brendan Cole, their partnership blossomed and, over the course of the next few years, they scooped most of the significant Latin titles in the world.

After the trials and traumas of the first series of *Strictly Come Dancing*, Dallerup picked herself up, dusted herself off and, most significantly, found herself a new professional dance partner in the shape of Ian Waite – who partnered Denise Lewis to near victory. And this time she was more fortunate in her dance partner, training with Roger Black who, unlike David Dickinson, was not only physically fit but also possessed of an innate sense of rhythm. This time, at least, she made it to the second half of the series, but again she was denied a crack at the final. Perhaps it'll be third time lucky for her in series three with her partner, top chef James Martin?

Brendan Cole

Of all the professional dancers in Strictly Come Dancing, *only one threatened to overshadow the 'real' celebrities in terms of press interest, and that was Brendan Cole.*

Apart from being a great dancer and very good-looking, in series one he pulled out the trump card – at least, in PR terms – of splitting up with his fiancée and dance partner, Camilla Dallerup, and sparking rumours of a relationship with his co-competitor, Natasha Kaplinsky. There was no doubt that they were the best dancers on the floor – but their runaway success with the public owed as much to the Cole-Kaplinsky chemistry, and the acres of press coverage it attracted.

Brendan Cole is the opposite of the clichéd image of the male ballroom dancer as a wooden, sexless dummy. A strapping six-foot-one New Zealander who started off working on building sites, he arrived at the BBC oozing sex appeal, singing the praises of the rumba 'because it's two bodies trying to create a moment', and a track record to prove it. His professional relationship with Camilla Dallerup had quickly become personal. 'We'd only just started dancing together, and I flew to Denmark to train for the Blackpool championships. We both agreed that the relationship was to be purely professional. I stayed in Camilla's flat in a bed on the opposite side of the room. That lasted five minutes.'

Dancing together, Cole and Dallerup represented Denmark and New Zealand, but on *Strictly Come Dancing*, they were competing against each other. Their nine-year relationship foundered, and the press have speculated ever since about whether or not they will get back together. Whatever the truth of Cole's offscreen romancing, there was no doubt that he and Natasha Kaplinsky were magic on the dance floor. The first few weeks were tense: Kaplinsky was deeply unsure about the project, and Cole was, she said, 'gentle and polite at first, but after a few weeks he turned into a complete brute'. The caveman act worked. 'She was ridiculous,' he says, 'and I responded by treading on eggshells. But soon it was time to turn up the heat and get on with it.'

Cole and Kaplinsky danced their way to victory, and when he returned in series two, there was a high expectation that he would do the same with Sarah Manners. But they never gelled and there were rows, tears and recriminations. It didn't really matter: they were knocked out after five weeks, and Cole admitted that they had never got on as dancers.

Perhaps partnering a breakfast television presenter again, this time it's Fiona Phillips, will prove the magic formula for success?

The Presenters

'Our job is to bring the party into everyone's living room on a Saturday night,' says Tess Daly, co-presenter of *Strictly Come Dancing*. 'I see every aspect of the show: I'm out front with Bruce; I'm with the celebrities and the dancers, seeing their backstage jitters; I see the hair and make-up and wardrobe, and the most gratifying thing is seeing it all come together live, although I've probably seen more panic attacks than anyone else involved in the programme.'

For Daly and Bruce Forsyth, taking on the job of presenting *Strictly Come Dancing* was as much a leap of faith as for any of the contestants. They were going to be carrying an untried format; if it fell flat, they would be left with egg on their faces. 'Of course, we had no idea that the show would take off in the way it did,' says Forsyth, 'but we had faith. I wouldn't have done it otherwise. There's always an element of anxiety about a new format, but you have to go out there and sell it, get it across to the audience. From my point of view, it was good from the start, because there's plenty of opportunity for banter with the audience, with the dancers and with the judges. But it wasn't until the third or fourth week of the first series that the competitive side really got going, and then I knew we had a winner on our hands.'

Nobody saw the competition at such close quarters as Tess Daly. Interviewing the contestants backstage before they went on, or after they had performed, she witnessed the highs and lows of what quickly became a very intense experience for all concerned. 'Just before they go on to dance, we play the video of their week's training – and it's the first time they've seen it. Everyone crowds around backstage to see what the others have been up to, and that's when the competition really hots up. I've heard a lot of backbiting comments, nothing terribly bitchy, but you quickly realise that these people are serious about winning. Then, when they have to go on, the tension is incredible. I've never seen such fear. The celebrities are having to do something that doesn't come naturally to them, they've got to do it live in front of millions of people, and everything rests on that 90-second performance. That's their one chance. I really feel for them.'

The element of competition is vital,' says Forsyth. 'You've got a group of people who may never have danced a step in their lives – they might muck around in a disco from time to time but that's about it – and they don't want to go out there looking like a fool. They want to win. They start watching each other's performances, seeing who's got the edge in the quickstep or the tango. The athletes in particular are very competitive; that's the way they work. Denise Lewis had no dance background at all, but she was a very fit, conditioned woman who was determined to work on her technique until she felt she could win.'

Both Forsyth and Daly have their favourite moments from the competition: Christopher Parker running around with Hanna Karttunen on his back in the Paso Doble, Julian Clary shaking his maraccas in Blackpool, but the story that most stands out for both of them is the transformation of Natasha Kaplinsky. 'That was the most outstanding thing about the first series,' says Daly, 'watching Natasha turn from this terrified woman who was literally shaking with fear backstage into an elegant, confident dancer who could win the competition.'

'Natasha was petrified at first,' says Forsyth. 'She actually said to me backstage, "Bruce, please can you make sure that I get knocked out in the first week?" But then she started to enjoy herself, she realised that she could dance and she just romped away. That gave out such a positive message to people, showing that you can overcome your fears or your lack of experience and turn them into a real achievement – and that's exactly what *Strictly Come Dancing* is all about.'

And of course Kaplinsky enjoyed *Strictly Come Dancing* so much that, when Tess Daly was obliged to take time off to have a baby, she came in to present much of the second series. 'That was the best part of the whole experience for me,' she says, 'because I was back in my comfort zone! To be honest, I really enjoyed seeing other people go through the terror that I'd experienced. You could see them going on the same journey, all the fear about performing, all the physical discomfort, the anxiety at the time of voting, which is absolutely hideous, and you could think, My God, I did all that! Looking back on it, I found it hard to believe that I'd really put myself through it.'

But it was Kaplinsky's initial fear that endeared her to audiences and did as much to win her the first series as her evident dancing ability. 'The judges give their scores on technique, but the audience is responding to personality as well,' says Forsyth. 'I realised that during the first series, when somehow Christopher Parker was coming back week after week because all the mums and young girls were voting for him. They could see how hard he was trying, and how upset he was when the judges were mean to him, and they wanted to give the poor lad another

chance. Our job as presenters is to mediate between the expert opinion of the judges and the sympathies of the audience. That part of the show when the contestants come up and face the judges has become the moment when it all crystallises. The dancers have a chance to answer back, and emotions run high. The judges aren't afraid of being controversial or upsetting the dancers; they have to maintain their standards. I have to remind the audience of that sometimes, when they start booing: the judges are judging the dance, not the person. They're professionals. The public always has the chance to have their say, and that tension between the two voting systems is what's made *Strictly Come Dancing* such a success.'

The presenters' job doesn't just begin and end with the Saturday night show; *Strictly Come Dancing* makes almost as many demands on their time as it does on the dancers'. 'We spend three days in the week preparing, watching the films of rehearsals as much as possible, meeting with the producer, discussing the scripts, meeting with the band and practising our little dance routine that we do at the bottom of the steps. That has to be right, or we're going to look very bad! Anton [du Beke] has given me a couple of lessons; I want to look the part.'

'Saturday is a very long day,' says Forsyth, 'what with the results show later in the evening as well. By the time I get home I'm exhausted. Sundays are

a bit of a write-off. I get up in time for Sunday lunch, then I spend the afternoon reading the papers and sleeping. I've always appreciated lazy Sundays at home, ever since doing *Sunday Night at the London Palladium* for all those years in the 50s and 60s.'

For Forsyth and Daly, the experience of presenting *Strictly Come Dancing* has been entirely positive. 'All I ever get is positive remarks,' says Forsyth. 'I was doing a phone-in show on Radio 5 Live last year, and a woman called in to say how much her children loved it. They were three and four years old, and she said that from the moment they got up in the morning till they went to bed at night, they were fighting – apart from when *Strictly*

Come Dancing came on, and then they were dancing together. That says it all for me.'

For Daly, the *Strictly Come Dancing*-effect has gone even further. 'I was three months pregnant when the first series started, then I gave birth to my daughter, Phoebe, towards the end of 2004. I went back to present some of the second series when she was six weeks old, and she celebrates her first birthday at the start of the third series. She really is a *Strictly Come Dancing* baby, and everyone involved in the show has become like family to us. When I took her in to meet everyone, the wardrobe department gave her a little Paso Doble cape with her initial 'P' on the back. That's how much the show means to us all.'

Here Comes

Meet the people in power: the experts who can make all the training worthwhile, or can send the defeated contestants back to the dressing room...

Craig Revel Horwood

BACKGROUND Craig started as a dancer at home in Australia before moving to London and choreographing extensively for the West End stage. His many credits include the Olivier-nominated *Spend Spend Spend*. He also runs a furniture shop.

HIGHEST SCORE 10 to Jill in the series-two final

LOWEST SCORE 1 to Quentin in series two

WATCHES OUT FOR Personality (or lack of it)

MOST LIKELY TO SAY 'It's meant to be the dance of love, but it seemed as though it were the dance of desperation.'

Arlene Phillips

BACKGROUND One of Britain's best-known choreographers, Arlene made her name as the creator of 70s dance troupe Hot Gossip. She went on to choreograph *Saturday Night Fever* for the West End and Broadway, plus countless feature films and music videos for Queen, Elton John, Robbie Williams and many others.

HIGHEST SCORE Gave the show's first ever 10 to Natasha in series one, and to Jill and Denise in series two

LOWEST SCORE 1 to Quentin in series two

WATCHES OUT FOR Professional attitude, expressiveness in performance

MOST LIKELY TO SAY 'Where was the sex?'

the Judge

Len Goodman

BACKGROUND Len has been dancing all his adult life, and he now lectures and judges all over the word as well as running a dance school in Kent. But it nearly didn't happen: he started out determined to be a professional footballer.

HIGHEST SCORE 10 to Jill in the series-two final

LOWEST SCORE 3 to Quentin in the first show of series two

WATCHES OUT FOR Technique, good basic choreography and sticks to the rules

MOST LIKELY TO SAY 'You don't have to break the rules. I'm going to have to drop a point.'

Bruno Tonioli

BACKGROUND Long ago, Bruno was one of Bruce Forsyth's dancers and competed in *A Song for Europe* before starring in Elton John's 'I'm Still Standing' video and establishing himself as a choreographer. He's worked with Michael Jackson, Paul McCartney and French and Saunders.

HIGHEST SCORE 10 to Jill and Denise in the series-two final

LOWEST SCORE 3 to Quentin in series two

WATCHES OUT FOR A strong, storytelling relationship between the dancers

MOST LIKELY TO SAY 'It was like watching a Robin Reliant competing with a Ferrari.'

Len Goodman is the linchpin of *Strictly Come Dancing* – the man with the most experience of the ballroom and Latin-American worlds, a dancer, teacher and judge who brings technical and professional credibility to the show. 'When we were first talking about the format,' he says, 'there were a lot of people in the ballroom world who were miffed because there weren't going to be four professional ballroom judges on the panel. I had misgivings myself, I confess. But as the show got going, I realised that it worked. If there were four people like me, you'd get four identical scores, all based on technique. But with Arlene, Craig and Bruno you're getting a score based on a different approach. I'm looking at steps and holds – but Bruno is looking at the quality of the performance, Craig's looking for interaction and line, and Arlene is looking at the choreographic elements. There's no point in judging non-dancers purely on technique, it wouldn't be fair. We have to look at all the qualities that they bring to a performance.'

The tension between the stern verdict of the judges and the response of the voting audience is what makes *Strictly Come Dancing* tick – and that's something the judges are well aware of. 'We get a lot of flak from audiences who think we're being mean to their favourite celebrity, but I have to keep stressing that we're voting with our heads. It's up to the audience to vote with their hearts. We can only judge the dancing as it's done on the night – we're not looking at rehearsals or training or backstage footage. I've got a responsibility to the dance world to make sure that the best technique gets the best mark. It's not always easy, because obviously we're not seeing them all dancing together at the same time, so we can't rank them against each other. You have to start off giving average marks – sixes and sevens – until you get an idea of the overall standard, then you can start giving higher or lower marks as they're deserved.

'First of all, I'd be looking for decent posture, because if you've got that, you're half-way to being able to dance. Some people just don't have it, and you know that they'll never be able to do more than just flap around on the floor. Then I look at the

footwork, which is the basis of the dance. If the footwork's good, you can build up the choreography, but if it's not there, then it's like building a house without strong foundations – the walls are going to fall down. Finally, I look at the choreography, which should turn it all into a performance. A dance is like a garden: you've got to have the basic things, such as the grass and the trees – that's the posture and the footwork – but you also need the flowers, and that's the choreography. I know I come out with a lot of funny comments and analogies sometimes, about sausages and sizzle and all that, but all I'm trying to say is that you have to mix basic steps with good performance.'

Goodman has been such a success on *Strictly Come Dancing* that he was invited to judge the American version of the show, *Dancing with the Stars*. 'They called me up on the Friday, and said, "Would you be prepared to fly out to Los Angeles on Monday for a show that starts on Tuesday?" I nearly didn't go, but I'm glad I did, because

Dancing with the Stars turned out to be the biggest entertainment show on American television in years. The attention it got was incredible: there were six or seven network-news teams hanging around at the end of every broadcast, wanting to interview us. But I was stuck out there for seven weeks, getting homesick, so I was pleased when it was all over.'

Now Goodman and the rest of the panel are poised to deliver their verdict on another crop of celebrities – and he's coming to terms with a certain amount of fame himself. 'It's nice to be recognised, and people are never nasty to me because they think I'm a kind judge. Craig's the one who gets it in the neck – he's been accosted on trains and given a very hard time by people who think he's Mr Mean. It's nice for me to have a bit of fame, and it's done wonders for the dance business as a whole – but it's not going to turn my head. I was 60 when I got this job, and I'd been round the block a few times, so this is just the icing on the cake.'

Celebrities

Series Two

Roger Black

Roger Black certainly looked the part – fit athletic, and not averse to see-through shirts. But would the judges favour his footwork?

NAME Roger Black
DAY JOB Olympic 4000 metre sprinter, BBC sports presenter
DANCE PARTNER Camilla Dallerup
BEST DANCE The Foxtrot in week four, which scored 29 out of 40. Bruno compared Black to 'a matinee idol', while Craig said it was so perfect he was 'bored'.
WORST DANCE The Rumba in week six. Arlene said Black was dancing like 'a plank of wood'.
THE JUDGES SAID Arlene: 'You're gorgeous to watch, you have a lot of style, but I think you've got a long way to go.' Craig: 'Clumpy, ungainly, no bounce.'
HOW DID THEY DO? Knocked out after the sixth show.

There were two professional athletes in the second series of *Strictly Come Dancing*, and it might have seemed that they had an unfair advantage. Roger Black and Denise Lewis were never going to have any problems in the fitness department, unlike some who were puffing and panting when they came off the dance floor. But physical fitness does not ensure grace, rhythm or co-ordination. Training, however, proved a problem for Black, who was unable to commit to as his partner, Camilla Dallerup, would have liked. The lack of practice time became so frustrating that she had to accompany him on a trip to Cannes. It paid off. Black's dancing in the first few weeks of the show impressed the judges, and the scores were respectably high.

But just when everyone expected Black and Dallerup to soar into the upper echelons of the competition, something went wrong. Perhaps it was lack of practice, perhaps Black had just reached the limit of his dance talent, but in the sixth show both the Waltz and the Rumba were slammed by the judges. Even a clever bit of costume stagecraft, in which Black unhooked a huge floating panel of red chiffon over Dallerup's black dress, failed to tip the balance, and they were knocked out.

Black admitted that, as Dallerup had pointed out, he had a tendency to morph into *The Office*'s David Brent when under pressure, but he relished the competition. 'In the end, and this sounds corny, I have made a friend. Camilla and my wife, Jules, have become good friends, and that will last. There was nothing bad about doing *Strictly Come Dancing*.'

Sarah Manners

Stepping out from behind the casualty desk, Sarah Manners placed herself in the hands – and on the thighs – of Brendan Cole. Would she share in his second victory?

The *Strictly Come Dancing* experience isn't always easy for the girls from *Holby City* hospital. Verona Joseph was hampered by filming schedules in the first series, but Sarah Manners, who plays *Casualty*'s receptionist Bex, was in the middle of one of her heaviest-ever storylines in the show, in which her character was raped. Added to that, she quickly developed a tempestuous relationship with her dance partner Brendan Cole, which led to a spectacular falling-out. 'I saw him on the BBC2 show saying that dancing with me was like dancing with a brick wall,' said Manners, 'and I just burst into tears. Afterwards he was very apologetic, and wished he hadn't said it.' The pair managed to make up in time for their Paso Doble in the fourth week, a gothic extravaganza to Evanescence's 'Bring Me to Life', in which Manners revealed she would 'sacrifice myself on Brendan Cole's thighs'.

Training continued to be a problem, however, as Manners was stuck in Bristol filming *Casualty* when she should have been travelling up to London or Blackpool to train. In the first series, it was Brendan Cole's obvious chemistry with his dance partner Natasha Kaplinsky that led him to victory; but it seemed that was not going to be repeated in series two. After a troubled five weeks, and a disappointing Samba in which her heel got caught in her dress, Manners and Cole were knocked out. 'I'm not relieved,' said Manners, 'because that sounds like I was hating it. But I do feel like there's a weight lifted off my shoulders in that it was very stressful. I was very busy at work. I loved doing the show.'

NAME Sarah Manners
DAY JOB Actor, plays Bex Reynolds in *Casualty*
DANCE PARTNER Brendan Cole
BEST DANCE After a stormy week of public rows and minimal training, the bickering pair made up for long enough to execute an impressive Tango to 'Hernando's Hideaway', scoring 31.
WORST DANCE The Rumba in week two was 'stiff and icy' according to Bruno, and only scored 23, which was the same for their Samba in week five.
THE JUDGES SAID Len: 'You didn't have your heart in it.' Bruno: 'You have to let yourself go.' Arlene: 'Where was the sex?'
HOW DID THEY DO? Knocked out after the fifth show.

Julian Clary

Julian Clary wasn't the most obvious choice for Strictly Come Dancing. *He was the first to admit he couldn't dance and, to make matters worse, he made the claim that he had never touched a woman in his life.*

More seriously, his reputation as a loose cannon on live television had made entertainment producers nervous since some unfortunate remarks about Norman Lamont's red box at the British Comedy Awards in 1993. He was, without doubt, the wild card for the second series – and he ended up as one of its biggest stars.

From the start, when Clary was the first on the floor with Erin Boag, it was obvious that he was not a natural. 'I used to disco dance years ago,' he said. 'I came off the dance floor at a rough disco in Magaluf, and some vicious queen said, "Well, you realize you can't dance…". So I thought, all right, I won't dance any more. It was difficult to persuade myself to do this because I've always believed that I just can't dance.'

Less determined women than Erin might have given up at this point, especially after a discouraging 19 points from the judges – but the public realised that Clary was prepared to give it his best shot, and Boag responded by pushing him to his limits. As the weeks went by, Clary stayed in the competition, much to everyone's surprise. 'It's 100 per cent Erin. She's such a good teacher, she's so relentlessly, persistently positive, and she never shows any doubt that we might not quite be able to do something.' Clary's scores shot up to 27 for the second-week quickstep, and from then on the couple were in the running. He may not have been a dance floor natural, but the audience soon realised that Clary was capable of putting on a good show.

And his performance didn't end after the dance. His confrontations with the judges – particularly with Craig Revell Horwood – became a weekly treat. In the fourth week, after Revell Horwood's stinging assessment of his Paso Doble, Clary rounded on him with, 'You wouldn't know a Paso Doble if you sat on one!'. From then on, it was war. In the semifinal, Clary pointed out that Revell-Horwood was wearing 'too much foundation'. The climax came when Clary described the judge as a 'silly old queen'.

But in the final, Clary was outclassed. He Samba'd out saying, 'The show has brought real joy to my life.' And it has: within weeks he was back on live prime-time TV, presenting BBC1's lottery show.

NAME Julian Clary

DAY JOB Comedian

DANCE PARTNER Erin Boag

BEST DANCE 28 out of 40 for the sixth-week Waltz.

WORST DANCE A disastrous start with the first-week Cha Cha Cha, which scored only 19.

THE JUDGES SAID Bruno: 'Light as Tinkerbell!' Len: 'As soon as you got your maracas out, I knew we were in for a treat.'

HOW DID THEY DO? Miraculously made it to the second-series final.

Jill Halfpenny

Strictly Come Dancing *already had strong links with* EastEnders *before Jill Halfpenny joined the second series. 'I'd seen how hard Christopher worked, so I had no illusions it would be an easy ride.'*

'When they cast the second series, my name went into the hat along with five or six others; they knew that they wanted someone from *EastEnders* to be in it, because of the BBC1 connection.' Halfpenny was chosen, and from the very beginning of training it was clear that she had the potential to go all the way to the final.

'I did a bit of ballet and tap when I was a little girl, so I wasn't scared of dancing, and I had a good sense of rhythm. But I had never done ballroom before in my life, so when I started rehearsing with Darren [Bennett] I was really worried. It's funny how skills you learned in your childhood – in my case 15 years previously – come flooding back. Darren's a very strict, precise teacher, but I'm a hard worker too, and I like to get things right, so we clicked right from the start. I started taking it so seriously that I wouldn't even let him go for breaks, I just wanted to keep working.'

Halfpenny left *EastEnders*, in which she played Phil Mitchell's latest wife, Kate, the week before going into training for *Strictly Come Dancing*, a happy schedule coincidence that eased her workload considerably. 'The training was hard, but at least I could just concentrate on that, unlike other people who were juggling other jobs. But nothing could prepare me for the first show. Standing backstage waiting to go on was the most nerve-wracking experience of my life. I had complete and utter stage fright; I seriously wanted to run away when our names were announced. I felt completely out of my depth. That's never happened to me before.'

As the weeks went by, Halfpenny became more determined to get through to the final. 'It wasn't so much that I wanted to win; I just didn't want to miss a show. You put so much time and energy into learning those dances that it must be awful to be knocked out. The final was really hard for us; Darren had been ill and was really sick and dizzy on the night. We were both so tired – but adrenalin kicked in just when we needed it. The atmosphere at Blackpool was amazing, with everyone screaming and shouting, and it passed in a blur. I have to watch the video to remember what I did.'

NAME Jill Halfpenny
DAY JOB Actor in *Byker Grove* and *EastEnders*, more recently in the West End in *Chicago*
DANCE PARTNER Darren Bennett
BEST DANCE The judges gave their first (and so far their only) 40 out of 40 to Jill and Darren's Jive to 'I'm Still Standing' in the series-two final.
WORST DANCE 27 for their first-week Waltz
THE JUDGES SAID Arlene: 'As a choreographer, I bow to you, Jill. The warmth was phenomenal.'
Len: 'I'm overwhelmed. Best dance of the series.'
HOW DID THEY DO? Winners of the second series and of the Champion of Champions Christmas special programme.

Diarmuid Gavin

Diarmuid Gavin may have green fingers – but it soon became apparent that he also has two left feet. Could the bad boy of gardening cultivate new talents on the dance floor?

NAME Diarmuid Gavin
DAY JOB Garden designer and TV presenter
DANCE PARTNER Nicole Cutler
BEST DANCE Despite a hamstring injury sustained on another dance floor, Gavin managed a personal best of 17 out of 40 for his Paso Doble in the fourth show.
WORST DANCE Where to begin? The first three dances polled only 12 out of 40 apiece.
THE JUDGES SAID Craig: 'Crude and lumpy.' Bruno: 'You're holding a beautiful girl, not a potted plant. A Quickstep is supposed to be like a soufflé, light and fluffy. This was a spotted dick.'
HOW DID THEY DO? Knocked out after the fourth show.

Diarmuid Gavin never had very high hopes of his chances on *Strictly Come Dancing*. Even during the training, he complained, 'It's not working. I'm fat, hairy and pale. I'm from Dublin and I'm not black so I haven't got any sense of rhythm. At the end of the day, I can't bear to look at myself in the mirror.' Being white and Irish isn't much of a reason for being unable to dance – ask Michael Flatley – but having absolutely no sense of rhythm whatsoever certainly doesn't help. Gavin's dance partner, Nicole Cutler, was visibly frustrated in rehearsals by his inability to hear the beat, or to make his body move in anything like time. But, as it turned out, Quentin Willson was even worse – and so Gavin managed to stay in the show until the fourth week.

When the axe finally fell, Gavin was 'disappointed and embarrassed' – but he could have taken comfort in the fact that his considerable fan base had kept him in for so long. Ultimately he accepted that the judges may have had a point. 'They're probably right,' he said. 'I felt it should have been about people who couldn't dance, learning progressively, week by week. But I didn't hear any of that in what they were saying.'

It was Gavin's self-consciousness that did for him. Nicole Cutler said he was much better without the camera on him. 'I can't understand this man,' she said. 'He's extremely sexy, he's loved in Britain and Ireland, and housewives adore him, but he's the most self-conscious person.' Something good came out of the experience, though. Gavin's eight-month-pregnant wife, Justine, spent the entire series 'rolling around on the carpet laughing at me.'

Esther Rantzen

Before Strictly Come Dancing, *Esther Rantzen described herself as 'a little old lady with a hump' and her clumsy gait and long feet as like 'an elephant on skis'. Five weeks pressed against Anton du Beke changed all that.*

He ruthlessly straightened her shoulders, lengthened her neck, and taught her to glide round the floor. The result? Esther waltzed elegantly to 'Moon River', swooping and dipping in a dress to suit Ginger Rogers. Arch-bitch Arlene Phillips approved her first performance as classy and professional.

Things started well for Rantzen and du Beke with an elegant waltz in the first week but their second week rumba was a mess. 'The Rumba is "the dance of love", and much as I loved Anton I was terrified by his commands to push out my bust and stick out my bum. I had to do something to distract him, so I bought myself a cheap red wig.' She christened it 'Sharon' in honour of Mrs Osbourne. It did the trick and the audience voted to keep her in. The third week she had to dance the Tango, with its sharp, staccato movements. Terrified that Sharon might be shaken loose, she abandoned the lucky wig and put a garter on her thigh instead. Rantzen strutted her stuff in a Tango that Craig Revel Horwood described as 'technically an absolute disaster, but dramatically triumphant'. Sadly, it was too late, and low scores from the judges and weak public support booted her out. Rantzen, however, was still a winner. 'It changed my life,' she says. 'After the show I took Sharon to my hairdressers, they copied the colour and I've been a redhead ever since. Whenever I'm at a supermarket check-out people say, "Aren't you lucky, you're a natural dancer." I never tell them my dancing is as natural as my hair!' All the exercise lost four inches off her waist, 'My children say I look ten years younger. Why bother with a gym when you can go dancing with Anton du Beke?'

NAME Esther Rantzen OBE
DAY JOB TV presenter, creator and chair of Childline
DANCE PARTNER Anton du Beke
BEST DANCE The Waltz in week one impressed the judges, who gave them 24 points.
WORST DANCE Fancy footwork got the better of Esther in the second and third shows; the Rumba and the Tango both polled a poor 16.
THE JUDGES SAID Arlene outbitched herself for Rantzen's Rumba. 'It's meant to be the dance of love,' she said, 'but it seemed as though it were the dance of desperation.'
HOW DID THEY DO? Knocked out after the third show.

Aled Jones

He was used to walking in the air, but had stayed away from the dance floor. Then Aled Jones amazed everyone by making it all the way to the semi-final.

'I really couldn't dance before I did the show,' says Aled Jones. 'I was so bad that I didn't even dance on my wedding night, I just propped up the bar.' But after missing out on a shot at the first series of *Strictly Come Dancing* – he was touring Australia at the time Jones was 'chomping at the bit' when the producers asked him to come back for the second. 'It was the attraction of learning a new craft, after singing all my life. Everyone laughed at the thought of me dancing – my daughter in particular thought it was funny – but I knew that at the very least it would teach me to move a bit, and get me fit.' The experience did far more than that: during the course of training, Jones lost two and a half stone, more than anyone else who has featured in the show.

'I started off as a complete novice with no ideas about dance at all. To make matters worse, I was on a 36-date UK tour throughout the series, so we had to fit training in around my schedule. Lilia [Kopylova] had to follow me all over the country, which made it hard for her. Our first lesson was in Ely, and she was absolutely formidable. I had to learn a Cha Cha Cha, to Ricky Martin's 'She Bangs', and I came out of there thinking, well, there goes my *Songs of Praise* contract. This is far too sexy. In fact, the *Songs of Praise* audience turned out to be my best supporters. I think they appreciated seeing the real me, with the odd swear word. It's been liberating from that point of view.'

To everyone's surprise, not least his own, Jones turned out to be a decent dancer and a favourite with judges and viewers alike. He fought through round after round, despite some hairy moments. 'During our Jive, I completely forgot the steps, and had to stand there punching the air. Lilia actually forgot to smile for five seconds. It was real brown-pants time – like when I forgot the words to 'Memory', of all things, at a Royal Variety Performance in front of the Queen.'

Despite being knocked out in the semi-final, Jones returned for the Christmas special. 'I wore a white bejewelled catsuit. My friends and family keeled over. But I got that weight off, and it's staying off. That's just one of the lasting effects of the show. I'm a lot more confident on stage now. And for the first time in my life, people come up to me and talk about something other than the bloody Snowman. It's about time.'

NAME Aled Jones
DAY JOB Singer and television presenter
DANCE PARTNER Lilia Kopylova
BEST DANCE Overcoming injury and memory-loss in the Jive in week three, 32 out of 40.
WORST DANCE A disappointing Foxtrot in week four scored only 25.
THE JUDGES SAID Len: 'All balls and no heels.' Craig: 'Laboured and lumbering.'
HOW DID THEY DO? A surprise departure from the semi-final.

Denise Lewis

The Olympic heptathlete needed something to cheer her up after injury forced her to pull out of Athens 2004. But was Strictly Come Dancing *just what the doctor ordered?*

'Athens was soul-destroying,' says Denise Lewis, whose Olympic ambitions were dashed when injuries forced her to pull out of the competition. 'I needed something that would take my mind off things and make me laugh. That's why *Strictly Come Dancing* came at such a good time. I didn't have to dwell on my disappointment any more. I could throw my energy into something completely different.'

And that's exactly what she did. Training with her dance partner Ian Waite turned her from a lean, mean athletic machine into a vision of grace and agility on the dance floor. 'This may sound corny, but I've always wanted to be a dancer. Ever since I was a little girl I've loved jiggling around.' That 'jiggling' took a 12-year-old Lewis on to local stages in the Midlands, where she tap-danced in sequins to 'Singin' in the Rain'. But eventually she had to choose between dance and athletics, and the rest is history. 'I had to make my mind up, and I knew deep down that dancing wasn't my strongest point.'

Waite drew out her latent talent though, and within weeks of a nerve-wracking début Lewis was gliding around with the best of them. Bruno Tonioli likened her to a panther, and throughout successive rounds Lewis's technique improved, along with her confidence. Lewis went into extra training – once an Olympian, always an Olympian – and took ballet lessons to improve her poise. 'I learned so much from those classes. I began to understand what it means to finish off with your fingers, which I hadn't got before.' The training paid off, and in the semi-final Lewis tangoed her way into the judges' good books.

'They announced that Julian was going through, and I thought, 'that's it, we're out, time to go home," she says. 'Then they called Aled's name. I was in shock. I couldn't even be happy I was going through.' After being pipped at the post by Jill Halfpenny in the final, Lewis revealed that she nearly hadn't made it on to the dance floor. 'I suffer from an excruciating stomach disorder called Irritable Bowel Syndrome. It's caused by stress, and so the first time I was due to perform in front of millions of viewers, I was sure an attack would happen. We stepped out, the music began and – nothing. I hope it means I've finally overcome it.'

NAME Denise Lewis MBE

DAY JOB Olympic heptathlete

DANCE PARTNER Ian Waite

BEST DANCE An exceptional 38 out of 40 for the final Quickstep.

WORST DANCE Their Jive to Rachel Stevens's 'Some Girls' only scored 25 in the third week.

THE JUDGES SAID Bruno: 'The poise of a panther playing with her prey.' Craig: 'Very, very exciting. I can't take my eyes off you.'

HOW DID THEY DO? A few points short of overall victory in the final.

Carol Vorderman

Some people sit back and let the judges' comments wash over them. Not Carol Vorderman, who, after a shock exit in the second week, hit back with some comments of her own.

NAME Carol Vorderman MBE
DAY JOB *Countdown* presenter, all-round TV personality and maths whizz
DANCE PARTNER Paul Killick
BEST DANCE 22 out of 40 for their first-week Waltz. They lost marks on technique.
WORST DANCE 20 out of 40 for their second-week Rumba – during which Vorderman sustained a cartilage injury. Skin-tight, flesh-coloured outfits didn't even win over the judges.
THE JUDGES SAID Arlene: 'I didn't see any connection between you. You lacked emotion.'
HOW DID THEY DO? Knocked out after the second show.

Before the start of series two, there were plenty of people who thought Carol Vorderman could walk off with the *Strictly Come Dancing* trophy. She was, after all, well known for her love of parties and sparkly dresses; surely dancing would be second nature? She could also rely on her massive *Countdown* audience to get the votes in. But, in the event, she and partner Paul Killick were booted off after the second show. What went wrong?

Writing in the press after she left the show, Vorderman let rip with an invective that left no doubt as to where she thought the trouble was. She accused Arlene Phillips of 'undisguised animosity' and described her as 'Sharon Osbourne, without the charm'. This led to a war of words between the two women, but it was too late to save Vorderman, whose chance of dance glory had gone.

It's a shame because from the two performances she gave, she had what it takes to go a lot further. But perhaps it was just as well she took an early bath, because an injury in the second week meant that training could have been a problem. She tore some cartilage beside her ribcage during the Rumba, and, despite smiling through the rest of the show, she went straight to casualty the next day. 'Paul's nickname is "the Killer",' she said, 'and now I know why!'

It was a painful end to a beautiful friendship. 'When I first met Paul,' she said, 'he introduced himself, "Hi, I'm Paul. Put your leg around my waist, hold the back of my neck, and lean back as far as you can when I tell you to." Twenty minutes later I hobbled away like Nora Batty's bandy sister.'

Quentin Willson

Some people are natural dancers. Some people can learn to dance through effort and training. And then there's Quentin Willson...

'My wife said it would be fantastic,' said Quentin Willson when he went into training for *Strictly Come Dancing*. 'I think she was hoping that it would make me less clumsy and stop me stepping on the dog. I really am the worst dancer.' This was not false modesty. Despite the best efforts of Willson's long-suffering training partner, Hazel Newberry, nothing on earth was ever going to turn the ugly duckling of the dance floor into an elegant swan.

Willson tried hard in training, but from the moment he stepped out for his first-week Cha Cha Cha it was obvious that he was not long for the show. The judges served up some of their most withering put-downs (see below), and, unfortunately, the viewers agreed. 'I think I now know that I am to dancing what Frank Bruno is to English literature,' said Willson when the verdict was delivered. 'Builders on the street have been congratulating me on my bravery. The most disappointing thing is that I let Hazel down.'

But Willson was a good loser, and he chalked the whole thing up to experience. 'When I was first asked to do this, my initial reaction was yes, of course, I can do it. It's just a question of putting one foot in front of the other. But I found it the most difficult thing I've ever done. I've loved every single minute of it, and I'm going to miss it. But success in life is knowing what your limitations are.' So Willson went back to stepping on the dog – but seven pounds lighter, and minus two inches on his waist.

NAME Quentin Willson
DAY JOB *Top Gear* presenter
DANCE PARTNER Hazel Newberry
BEST/WORST DANCE There was only one, the Cha Cha Cha – not the easiest dance for a novice to begin with. The judges only managed a grand total of eight marks – the lowest score to date on *Strictly Come Dancing*.
THE JUDGES SAID Craig: 'Britain's worst dancer!' Bruno: 'It was like watching a Robin Reliant with a Ferrari.'
HOW DID THEY DO? Knocked out after the first show.

A Few Moments from
Series Two

The Way You Look Tonight

While the dancers are busy in the studio mastering the footwork that will, they hope, lead them to glory, there's a huge team of hair and make-up artists, costume designers and stylists preparing the elaborate, often expensive outfits that will help all the contestants to make an impact on judges and audiences. As much as it's a dance show, Strictly Come Dancing has also become a byword for glamour – and each and every look that twirls across the floor is the result of weeks, sometimes months of preparation.

It starts with the costumes – and these aren't just pretty off-the-peg dresses and suits that you might wear to a party. Dance clothes are complicated bits of technical kit that have to look good (and not rip!) while the wearer puts them through the most demanding of workouts. 'If you just wore normal clothes for *Strictly Come Dancing*, you'd be in big trouble,' says Su Judd, costume stylist for the show. 'The men have special dance trousers made of a high-grade stretch polyester, cut very wide in the crotch and with a very high waist – otherwise the shirt would come out, and the trousers would split at the seams. Even with the specialist dance trousers, we do have the odd accident – so the men wear black underpants, just in case. We don't want to see any flashes of white! The trousers are long in the leg too, so that we don't

see socks or bare legs. The jackets are amazing: the shoulders are made so that even when the arms are up in the air, they look flat – ordinarily you'd get a lump – and the arms are extra-long so they don't ride up. There isn't actually a waistcoat; the bit at the front is just holding everything in place.

'The women's costumes are even more specialised. All those dresses that you see are basically built round a made-to-measure leotard that the dancer just steps

Go with the 'fro: Denise Lewis works the wig for her series-two Jive with Ian Waite.

into. Some of them have zips, but most of them are just lycra with the rest of the dress attached over it. The leotard is always made in the same colour as the dress, so you won't notice it when the dress moves. The leotards stretch every which way, they move with you as you dance and they support you in all the right

places. If you wore a normal dress and you were thrown back in a tango, for instance, your chest would fall out. These hold you in, nice and firm!'

Su Judd's job as costume stylist is to bring all the different clothing elements together – and then persuade the contestants to wear them! 'I work closely with the designers and makers of the clothes, but to be honest the major part of my job is convincing the celebrities to dress the part, and to reassure them that they're going to look great. I know all the rules – I can do the Trinny and Susannah thing – so they trust me to a certain extent. Whatever size or shape they are, whether they've got a big bust or short legs, I'm going to make them look good. But this isn't just fashion styling, this is getting people into clothes that feel and look very unusual, and they don't necessarily have the confidence to put them on. The professional dancers are used to wearing this gear in their working lives, but for the celebrities it's a big leap of faith, and they're terrified of looking stupid. It was particularly difficult with the first series of *Strictly Come Dancing*: nobody

The long and the short of it: Carol Vorderman (left, with Paul Killick) and Lesley Garrett (right, with Anton du Beke) were among the wardrobe department's more willing subjects.

knew if it was going to be a hit or not, and they didn't want to make fools of themselves. It's easier now we've done two very successful series, I must say!'

Some stars are easier to dress than others. 'Believe it or not,' says Judd, 'the person we had the biggest problem with in the first series was Natasha Kaplinsky. She would be the first to admit that she had serious misgivings about the show. She's a newsreader, a serious journalist in a predominantly male world, and she did not want to blow her credibility by coming out looking like a fruit salad. When we first met, I took along a drawing that the designers had done, and a selection of beautiful fabrics; we sat down in her dressing room at the BBC and she just burst into tears, "I can't do it, I can't do it!" I really thought we were going to lose her at that stage – which would have been such a shame, because she's got such a great figure we couldn't wait to start dressing her. I knew she'd look good even in the most extreme outfits – and dance costumes are pretty full-on – but she was terrified. So I talked to her about the kind of clothes she likes to wear, and we went right back to very simple, safe looks to build up her confidence at the start of the show. Then it was just a question of working with her to achieve something we were both happy with.

'The fittings started out with Natasha wearing things that covered her from top to toe – then we'd get a pair of scissors and start cutting off a bit here, a bit there – literally while she's wearing it. Natasha hasn't got much chest, she's tall and elegant, so she's crying out for plunge necks and high splits – but that took some work. Brendan [Cole, Kaplinsky's dance partner] would be there supervising – the men can be very controlling about what the women wear, but I didn't mind in Brendan's case because he does have a good eye. Every week, we managed to get Natasha to wear a little less and show a little more. The breakthrough came in the fourth week, when we went to Blackpool and she was dancing the Jive. The dress was black, with cobalt-blue shoes, fringing at the hem and stones down the tights. The key to the Jive is seeing the legwork, so when we were fitting it, we cut the skirt

really high. Natasha was desperately worried, but we knew it looked good, and Brendan was confident that she could do the dance properly. She nearly refused to go out in it, but by that time it was too late, the dress was made and everyone thought she looked great. We persuaded her at the eleventh hour, she went out and she did really well. For the first time, we realized that she was enjoying herself. After that, she was much more relaxed about what she'd wear. Mind you, we had taken along a bit of extra fringing so that we could lower the skirt, just in case she really wouldn't wear it – but she didn't need to know that! In the next few weeks, she just took flight. Her confidence was reflected in the clothes that she wore.'

CREATING THE DESIGNS

Outfits for the celebrities have to be designed well in advance, as making and fitting them is a costly process. For the women's dresses, the show employs Chrisanne Limited, the UK's leading dancewear makers. 'All the designers and makers at Chrisanne are ex-dancers,' says Judd, 'so they know exactly what will work. I go along for a consultation and we pick out colours and fabrics for the whole show, based on what's fashionable that season. Then they design the dresses for all the celebrities in all the dances. Those drawings go back to the female celebrities, they

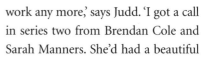

pick out the ones they like and they're sent back to Chrisanne to be redrawn. Once everyone's happy with the design and the colours, they make the dresses up. They're expensive: each dress costs anything from £1500 to £2500 apiece and is worn only once before being sold on. Chrisanne bears the cost of making it, then we hire the dress from them for a fee, then they take it back, remake the gusset, clean it and sell it on – there's a massive market for those dresses in the dance world, particularly in the US and Japan.'

Because *Strictly Come Dancing* is a live show with a competitive element, nobody quite knows from week to week what's going to be required on the night. Chrisanne's designs may have to be abandoned or completely reworked according to the dancers' needs – and that's no small undertaking when the garments are so intricate. The finishing touches of sparkle are all applied by hand just before the dress is worn. Chrisanne sends the dresses out to a group of specialists who hand-glue every single stone to the fabric – and that can be thousands on a single dress. But even with such attention to detail, the best-laid plans can always go awry.

'You never know when the dancers might change a routine, and suddenly the dress doesn't work any more,' says Judd. 'I got a call in series two from Brendan Cole and Sarah Manners. She'd had a beautiful gold-and-turquoise dress designed for their Paso Doble, it was agreed on and half made, and then on the Sunday night I found a message at home saying. "Please don't be angry, but we've changed the routine." They'd decided to dance to 'Bring Me to Life' by Evanescence, which is quite a dark, gothic song, and they wanted to do a sort of Dracula routine. Well, gold and turquoise wasn't going to work for that! I put a stop on that dress, then grabbed a black outfit that Hanna had worn in a demonstration dance and just cut it in half, pinned bits in, draped a bit of fabric over Sarah's bum, stuck stones over the joins. Brendan just wore black trousers and a black bolero jacket, bare-chested. And it worked! But that's a very rare occurrence, I'd like to point out, just in case the dancers are reading this.'

Other factors can demand quick thinking in the costume department, such as rapid weight loss. something that affected quite a few of the celebrities as they went through intense training. Aled Jones lost two stone in the second series, which meant trousers had to be taken in and

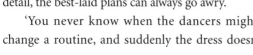

> 'The fittings started out with Natasha wearing things that covered her from top to toe – then we'd get a pair of scissors and start cutting off a bit here, a bit there – literally while she's wearing it.'

shirts bought in smaller sizes. But the biggest challenge came from Lesley Garrett, who lost 16lb in the first series – and totally changed shape as a result. 'She had to be refitted every week. Those dance leotards that the women wear are made to measure – they have to be a perfect fit, otherwise things will fall out – and Lesley's bum and bosom kept shrinking and shrinking. In the first show, she was worried about looking mumsy, and we'd done a lot of work on the dresses to make sure that she didn't look top heavy. There's no underwiring in a leotard, they hold your boobs in by squashing them, basically – so we had to devise something that would give Lesley adequate support while not letting her pop out in the middle of a dance. Then the weight started to come off, and we were remaking and refitting every single week. She was so pleased with her black and white foxtrot dress that she bought it from us, and she wears it in her own stage show now.'

The men's outfits are far less labour intensive than the women's – but there are still plenty of challenges for Su Judd and her team. 'Men are, generally speaking, very conservative about what they're prepared to wear. They don't want to look camp.

Christopher Parker, in the first series, was terrified of looking like a prat; he's got a reputation as Mr Cool, and a big fan following, and he didn't want to endanger that. I put him in designer gear all the way through. The men all have their special dance trousers, but I'll buy their shirts for them; I took him a large selection of beautiful designer stuff from Harrods and just let him choose what he liked best, because I could see that his confidence needed building up. He picked out a Roberto Cavalli shirt, and he had a jacket with a snake in stones down the back. He was the only one who would agree to wear any sparkle at first – and I think that had something to do with the nice shirts I gave him. Some of the men's stuff comes from high-street shops like Zara or Top Man; it doesn't have to cost a fortune. After that, Christopher didn't mind wearing stones. I'd shown him pictures of David Beckham wearing a white shirt with stones all over it, and he was much happier. Some of the other men will play the game – Roger Black and Martin Offiah let me send them out in some very revealing outfits, but when you've got a body like each of them I suppose it's easier. But some of the men wouldn't do a thing. Diarmuid Gavin wouldn't undo buttons or wear sparkle. Once I pinned a

glittery shamrock to his jacket just before he went put – you have to be sneaky.'

One person who didn't need much persuading to glam it up was Julian Clary. 'During his career, he's worn just about everything. I actually had to tone him down. I didn't want him going out there looking bizarre; the men in the dance world consider themselves butch and manly, and they wouldn't be happy if they thoght that Julian was sending them up. Fortunately, Julian is very fit and elegant, and it didn't take much to send him out looking like Fred Astaire. He looks good in suits. He always wanted a bit of sparkle, but it was restrained; it was very important that he didn't overshadow Erin. I liked him best in the more conservative outfits, the midnight-blue suits with a few stones. He looked very Hollywood.'

PREPARING FOR THE SHOW

Su Judd's team of eight dressers, plus assistants and designers from Chrisanne, has a huge job on the day of the live show. 'Every pair of dancers has a dresser assigned to them, plus we have Bruce and Tess, the band, the singers and the judges to take care of. I go into the studio on the Friday and make sure everything is in place – from the clothes right down to the last bit of feather or trim – so when we start dressing them on Saturday there are no last-minute surprises. We let them see the clothes when they're rehearsing, but they can't dance in them, because they're so easily stained or ripped. After the morning rehearsal they have lunch, then we dress them in time for the full dress rehearsal in the afternoon. I sit up in the control room, watching it on the monitors so that I can be certain it looks good on TV – there's still time to make any last tweaks, or to repair things that get damaged. One week, Diarmuid stood on Nicole's skirt and ripped the fringe off; that was sewn back on in the nick of time.'

During the live broadcast, and in the period before the later results show, the contestants stay in their

costumes but are encouraged to keep away from food and drink. 'I try to put capes over them, in case they drop something, and I ask them not to dance, because we don't want any accidents. We spend a lot of that time in between the shows making small adjustments, telling them they were fantastic, basically keeping everyone in good spirits. We're not just dressers, you know. Half the time we're psychiatrists as well.'

FINISHING TOUCHES

When the clothes are on, the dances rehearsed, the band ready to strike up and the lights in position, the very last piece of the puzzle to be fitted into place is the hair and make-up. It may come last but, says make-up and hair designer Gilly Popham, it's often the first thing to be noticed. 'When the dancers step out on to the floor, people instantly take in the way they look – and that means the face and the head first. If that doesn't make a good impression, it can let everything else down the costume, the dancing, the whole show.'

Erin Boag, Lilia Kopylova, Darren Bennett and Anton du Beke get ready for our photo shoot, with hairdressers Anna Winterburn and Brendon Midson, and make-up artists Jo Jenkins and Christine Bateman.

Hair and make-up can make or break a routine, and it's vital that they should not only fit in with the style of the dance but suit each individual as well. 'Some of them are willing to put themselves entirely into our hands,' says Popham. 'Denise Lewis, for instance, would let us do crazy things with her hair, putting in extensions, getting her to wear wigs and jewels. But some of them have a very particular look that they're unwilling to depart from. That can be difficult when you're trying to get them ready to get out and do a certain type of dance.'

The style that Popham and her team of artists employ on *Strictly Come Dancing* is, she says, 'traditional dance make-up modified for television. You can't go for the usual dance make-up – it's far

too strong. It's designed to be seen from the back row of an auditorium, so you have great thick lines around the eyes, the hair practically glued to the head. But on *Strictly Come Dancing*, these people are going to appear on screen in single close-ups, and we're going to see them backstage being interviewed. We can't send them out there looking like freaks. That was one of the problems with the old *Come Dancing* series: they didn't adapt the make-up enough, so the dancers looked like really strange mannequins. We tone the look down so it's closer to fashion make-up than stage – but it still has to look suitably dramatic. It's a very fine balance.'

Hair and make-up has to work with every other element of the performance, co-ordinating and emphasising elements present in the music, the choreography, the costume and the lighting. 'The first thing I do is talk to the producer about the overall look of the show, the sets, the lighting and the clothes, so that we're all aiming for the same style. In the first series, we went for a very high-fashion, glam look, which was reflected in the make-up. The second series was a bit more elegant, more Hollywood, with period elements from the 20s through to the 50s. There's always a guiding principle to what we do, and it's the finishing touches like the colour of nails or the use of hair ornaments that really set the tone.'

Getting the show ready is a massive task: it's not unusual for Popham and her team to have 40 people to prepare. It's not just the dancers – there are the presenters, the judges, the singers and the guest artists as well. 'We get in at nine in the morning, and we work non-stop into the night. We might get a 20-minute break if we're lucky. The team that I have working for me are all top stylists, who see this as a great challenge.'

The team meets half an hour before they start work to check through the programme for the day; Popham issues them with a call sheet that details every single make-up and hair look that they need to create. 'Then we get cracking. First of all we do their hair – and it's not unusual to be sewing in hairpieces or switches, which takes a lot of time. They have to be very firmly fixed – you can't have false hair flying off in the middle of a dance – but it also has to move naturally on camera, so we can't glue it down. After that we just work our way through everyone. The contestants can be in make-up for up to two and half hours. It's not like going out for the night; we do absolutely everything. We paint their nails, sometimes we do false nails, there are false

Julian Clary was only too happy to look the part, and Erin was brave enough to allow him to practise his make-up skills, as well as his dancing skills, on her!

eyelashes to stick on, sometimes there's fake tan to apply. And the men aren't any easier – there's a lot of general grooming that you have to do on a man. Shaving the back of the neck so it looks tidy, trimming the hair, the eyebrows, the facial hair, nose, ears, the lot. If they're baring their chest or arms we have to make them look good; I spent hours putting cream on Martin Offiah's body so that he went out shining. In the first series, we used a lot of that – the shiny look was very fashionable at the time, to the extent that some people looked as if they'd been dipped in a vat of Vaseline.'

Popham's job doesn't end when the show starts either; there's always something to be done. 'We're the first people the dancers see when they arrive in the morning, and we're the last ones they have contact with before they go on stage. We're there with them in the wings, powdering them, touching up lips, boosting their confidence. They have to feel that they look fantastic before they go on, and so that's our job too.'

The professional dancers are used to wearing full warpaint and going out in front of an audience, but for some of the celebrity contestants it's a new and unnerving experience. 'Even the actors and entertainers find it weird,' says Popham, 'because they're not going out there to do their usual job. They're appearing as themselves, so they want to look good, but they're doing something that they're not used to doing. The make-up is a mask to some extent, giving them confidence. But it can be very difficult to persuade them to take on the look we think they need.'

Just as Su Judd spends her time talking celebrities into showing more skin, Gilly Popham has to persuade the artists to adopt looks they wouldn't normally be seen dead in. 'Some of them are very open to change, but others have a fixed idea of how they should look, and they're not happy for us to mess around with that. It's part of their armour. Esther Rantzen, for instance, had a very definite idea of her own image, and when we first met she told me, "I will not wear false nails, false eyelashes or red lipstick." By the time the series was over, she was wearing the lot and she loved it. I think *Strictly Come Dancing* gave her a new idea of herself; she's a very attractive woman with a great face and a fantastic figure, and that really came across in the show. The turning point came when I wanted to get her into a red wig for her tango. She found one that she really liked, but it was far too expensive – I only have a small budget for hairpieces, and this would have really dented it. So Esther went and bought it herself, and she looked great in it. After she'd been knocked out of the show, she had her hair cut and coloured in the same style as the wig!'

Individual looks created by the team are specific not only to the dancers but also to the dances they're performing. 'The Latin dances generally have a more dramatic style, with lots of fake tan, smoky eyes, dark lips and swept-up hair with strong ornaments. The waltzes, however, are more understated and elegant. We're also influenced by what's on the catwalks and in the fashion magazines. I'm hoping to get a perfect blend between high fashion and the dance world, so I have to be quite inventive. We do experiment, mixing pigments and glitter into lip glosses or foundations; I know all the tricks of the trade, because I've been doing this a long time. And I'm inundated every week with requests for information about how I've achieved a certain look or effect. I could do my own book on the hair and make-up for *Strictly Come Dancing*, because people really do notice how the celebrities look.'

The high-glamour look characterised by *Strictly Come Dancing* has moved into the mainstream since the series began. 'I don't think we've necessarily influenced fashion,' says Popham, 'but we're certainly in tune with it. In the 80s, everyone wanted big hair and high-maintenance make-up. The 90s saw a reaction against that, and everything was very natural. Now I think people want glamour again;

if you look at the awards ceremonies on TV, you can see a lot of the looks that we've been using on the show.'

Strictly Come Dancing has a high-gloss style that's integral to the show's success, and that means that the hair and make-up team is never off duty. 'We're on our feet all day. At the start of the series we're sweet-talking people into trying new looks; at the end of the series, we're doing changes for them so that they can do two dances in a show. And there's endless maintenance; we have to get on to the floor when we can to touch up the presenters and judges. That's risky. Once a couple of make-up artists got caught on camera trying to powder the judges – they get so hot sitting under the lights. Tess Daly covered it brilliantly – she said, "There are two mad fans trying to nobble the judges!" – but now we have to be extra careful that we don't get spotted.'

At the end of the night, when the final dance has been danced and the results announced, the make-up team is on hand to help clean up the performers. 'We take out all the hair ornaments and pieces – we can't have them ripped out any old how – but the rest is up to them. They get a bag of cleansing products, and we leave them to it. We can't do everything.'

'At the end of the night, when the final dance has been danced and the final score announced, the make-up team is on call again to get the performers cleaned up and ready for bed'

Hanna Karttunen

There are surprises in Strictly Come Dancing, there are sometimes miracles, and then there is Christopher Parker. The fact that Hanna Karttunen managed to steer him to the final still ranks as the biggest surprise of the show, given that the young EastEnders star could barely dance a step when he began training.

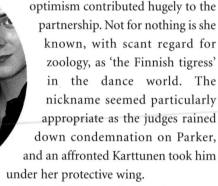

By the end of the show he could, perhaps, dance two steps – a tribute to Karttunen's perseverance – but the combination of their two personalities proved irresistible to viewers. We all know that young Mr Parker can mobilise huge armies of fans with one blink of his puppy-dog eyes, but Karttunen's own fiery charms and eternal optimism contributed hugely to the partnership. Not for nothing is she known, with scant regard for zoology, as 'the Finnish tigress' in the dance world. The nickname seemed particularly appropriate as the judges rained down condemnation on Parker, and an affronted Karttunen took him under her protective wing.

As Paul Killick's professional partner, Karttunen has won most of the significant titles in the Latin dance world – and they bowed out in spectacular style by retiring from competition during the series, and showing the world what they were made of with an unforgettable exhibition Samba.

For the rest of the series, she focused her energies on Christopher Parker, pulling him through each successive dance as if her life depended it, covering all his mistakes with fancy footwork, comforting him when the judges were mean. Somehow, it was enough. Week after week, even when they ended up at the bottom of the leader board, the public kept voting them back in to compete again.

Perhaps the effort was too much for her, as Karttunen did not return to dance in *Strictly Come Dancing.*

Anton du Beke

He's the gracious king of the ballroom floor and, thanks to Strictly Come Dancing, *he's also become the housewives' favourite.*

'I wish every woman on the planet could have half an hour with Anton du Beke,' gushed Lesley Garrett at the end of her stint on the first series of *Strictly Come Dancing*. While that may not be entirely practical, du Beke certainly made an impression on both his celebrity partners, not to mention the viewing public. Garrett liked him so much that she invited him to dance with her at gala concerts long after the show was finished. Esther Rantzen, du Beke's partner in series two, was similarly smitten. So keen was she on maximising their training time that she whisked him away on a three-day Caribbean cruise.

Du Beke is one of the stars of contemporary ballroom; with his professional partner, Erin Boag, he was named ICDT Classic Champion in 2003, and has a fistful of other awards and titles under his belt. He started dancing relatively late, at the age of 14, and at 17 decided to specialise in ballroom. He rose quickly through the ranks, and as well as being a champion, he became a sought-after teacher throughout the UK.

Du Beke emerged as one of the outstanding characters of the first series, largely due to his strictly-for-laughs friendship with Lesley Garrett. They fell on top of each other in rehearsals, they shouted at each other, they whipped up rivalry with the other contestants and appeared to be having the time of their lives. Du Beke admitted that 'This is the best thing I've ever done, and the highlight is being with Lesley every day.' That chemistry took them to the semi-finals, but despite superior dancing skills, they never made it to the final.

The second-series partnership with Esther Rantzen was never as fiery, but they clearly got on well. 'She's so wonderful,' said gallant du Beke. 'The Esther you've seen on telly over the last few years is nothing like the Esther you see in the studio. She's incredible fun.' Rantzen blossomed under du Beke's tutelage, but the judges and the public failed to respond.

In series three Anton du Beke is teamed up with a genuine redhead – will we see sparks between him and Patsy Palmer on the dance floor?

Ian Waite

Ian Waite's partnership with Denise Lewis enraptured the judges. 'Exotic! Sultry! Sexy!' raved Bruno – and it wasn't just Lewis's feline grace that caught his fancy.

Waite, a Latin champion since his teens, is a past master at whipping up passion on the dance floor. And it wasn't just during the competition that he brought feelings to boiling point. Sparks flew during training, too, as Waite goaded Lewis into working harder. 'Do you want to be good on Saturday, or not?" he snapped, forbidding her from taking her shoes off or resting. 'He's undergone some kind of metamorphosis,' complained Lewis. 'He's turned into Superbitch. I'm going to tear his head off by Wednesday.'

Fortunately for all concerned, there was no murder on the dance floor, and Waite and Lewis danced their way through to the final, where their only serious competition, at least in technical terms, was Jill Halfpenny and Darren Bennett. It was a close call – but ultimately the viewers' votes put Waite in second place.

It doesn't appear to have harmed his career. He has branched out into lecturing, demonstration dancing and big showbiz spectaculars. He's even made an instructional video with that other great ambassador of ballroom dancing, Angela Rippon!

In series three he'll be turning his teaching talents towards Zoe Ball – will her knowledge of dance music be a help or a hindrance?

Hazel Newberry

Like Kylie Jones in the first series, Hazel Newberry was no sooner in Strictly Come Dancing *than she was out. Her's was the misfortune to be partnered with Quentin Willson – easily the worst dancer of the 18 celebrity contestants to date, a man who made David Dickinson look like Nijinsky.*

This was hardly fair on Newberry, who's famous in the dance world for her elegance on the dance floor. She, after all, was likened by Bruno Tonioli to a Ferrari (while Willson, you will recall, was more of a Robin Reliant).

During a 12-year partnership with Christopher Hawkins, Newberry won most of the ballroom titles available to her, starting with the Open British Youth Modern Ballroom title in 1992 and never really stopping after that. They turned professional in 1997, and in 2001 and 2002 they won the British National Professional Dance Championships. Further international victories followed, and she was a natural choice for *Strictly Come Dancing*'s second series.

'The show came along at a really good time for me, after I'd just split with Christopher Hawkins,' she said. 'I'd seen the first series, and thought it was fantastic – and I knew it would be a great challenge for me.' Before the casting, Newberry had expressed her hope that she would be teamed up with a sports personality or 'someone like Paul O'Grady, someone who's game for a laugh and a total personality, willing to give it 100 per cent'. Unfortunately, this was not to be. Quentin Willson was none of those things, and he stomped them

out of the competition in a lumbering cha cha cha in the first week. Newberry was under no illusions.

'That routine had a few complicated steps,' she said, 'and I just thought, Nah – this isn't going to work.'

Lilia Kopylova

Diminutive Russian Lilia Kopylova (alias Mrs Darren Bennett) began dancing in her native Moscow at the age of nine, when her grandmother signed her up for ballroom lessons at school. Instantly hooked, she never looked back – and by the age of 15 she was already a ballroom and Latin champion.

As if this wasn't enough, she'd also won titles for figure skating and gymnastics; they take their competitions seriously in Russia. A chance meeting with Bennett's dancer brother Dale in Denmark brought her to England, where she had a 15-minute tryout with Darren – and they've been dancing (and living) together ever since.

So what's it like being a private couple, as well as a public one? 'We have two separate lives, professional and private,' says Kopylova. 'We may fight a bit on the floor during practice, but when we leave the dance hall, everything is behind us. It's gone, it's forgotten.'

Kopylova danced with Aled Jones in the second series, and he couldn't find enough good things to say about her during the course of training (not surprising, really, as she helped him to lose masses of weight). Her methods had been simple, but effective: she started off by calling him 'Five Bellies' and 'Shrek', until he got the message and laid off the pies. But when they were knocked out after the semi-final, she was shocked and, by her own admission, cried for three hours after the show. She rallied quickly, however, and threw her support behind her husband. 'Please,' she asked, 'all the votes for me, just give them to Darren.' It worked.

In series three she might well be making the same plea, but this time she won't be being so generous to her husband, the Darren she'll have in mind will be her dance partner, Darren Gough.

Off the dance floor, Kopylova is a down-to-earth Moscow– Sheffield girl who dreams of having a pet dog and lists as her favourite pastime, 'drinking games'.

Paul Killick

There's a bad boy in every gang, and Paul 'Killer' Killick established early in the first series that he was determined to fulfil that role in Strictly Come Dancing.

Bursting on to the floor in a leopardskin jacket, he executed a nifty Cha Cha Cha with Verona Joseph before lifting her up, spinning her around and depositing her on the floor. The judges gasped with disapproval (the dancers are supposed to keep a toe on the floor at all times), but still scored the performance highly, convinced that 'rules were made to be broken'. Killick was always going to be the loose cannon in *Strictly Come Dancing*, his reputation in the dance world rests upon his excellence in the Rumba and the Paso Doble – the most dramatic Latin dances.

Londoner Killick was moving to music before he could walk but a trip to the cinema took an unexpected turn when Killick's grandfather heard music and discovered the world-famous Peggy Spencer's Dancing School. Spencer, a veteran of the original *Come Dancing*, took Paul under her wing and nurtured what soon emerged as an extraordinary talent.

Killick trained throughout his teens until he turned professional in 1994. He then danced with Hanna Karttunen until their retirement; together they have a cupboard bursting with trophies. He didn't find it easy to adapt to the amateur competitiveness of the show, berating Verona Joseph, for her apparent lack of commitment. It didn't matter that she was working full time in *Holby*

City, Killick expected nothing short of 100 per cent. But what they lacked in technical perfection, they more than made up for in temperament. Killick's appearances were the most dramatic, explosive dances across the two series. When he and Hanna Karttunen did a farewell Samba, her in feathers, him

dressed in bright red, we could see what we'd missed by voting him off the show.

Unfortunately he didn't fare much better in the second series, when he was paired with Carol Vorderman, and crashed out of the competition after the second week. But Killick did quit the show on a high and soon opened his own London dance studio.

Kylie Jones

Blink and you'd have missed Kylie Jones – she was partnered with Jason Wood in the first series and was the first of the dancers to be knocked out of the show. That's a shame, because, on that slender showing, she was one of the more instantly likeable characters among the professional team.

She started dancing at the age of seven in her native Manchester, and by ten she was competing across the country. In 1989 she and her partner Stephen Sysum won the International Juvenile Ballroom Championship, and went on to even greater heights, winning the Open British Juvenile Ballroom championships three times in a row.

At 16, Jones changed partners and, with Jonathan Crossley, became twice World Amateur Ballroom Champions. They turned professional, taught and performed all over the world until dissolving the partnership in 2002. *Strictly Come Dancing* wasn't Jones's first TV appearance: at the tender age of 11 she was teaching John Leslie how to dance on *Blue Peter*, and later made an appearance on sports quiz *They Think It's All Over*.

Her experience on *Strictly Come Dancing* was short, but sweet. Jones and Wood clearly got on like a house on fire despite his obvious nerves and lack of dancing ability. When they were knocked out, Jones was gracious in defeat. 'He danced the best he could,' she said. 'He really couldn't have done any more.'

Lets Face the Music

One of the hardest – and most expensive – decisions that faced the producers of Strictly Come Dancing *concerned music. Would they use recorded music – familiar to audiences and competitors, but completely dead in terms of entertainment – or would they go to the trouble and cost of hiring a live band? 'There was never any doubt in my mind,' says executive producer Karen Smith. 'It had to be live. All the great entertainment shows have had a live band. and I wanted to capture that feeling of an old-fashioned dance hall, where a couple would go to hear a proper band. If we were going to appeal to a big audience, and give that feeling of genuine entertainment, it was vital to get the best in the business.'*

So Smith hired Laurie Holloway, veteran jazz musician, composer, arranger and one of the few people in the world who can claim to have worked with both Judy Garland and Lily Savage. 'My agent called me one day and said he'd just been asked if I'd do *Strictly Come Dancing*,' says Holloway. 'I said, You must be joking!' But we found out more about it, and eventually I got hooked on the idea. Now it takes over my life for six months of the year.'

Holloway put together a big band – three trumpets, three trombones, four woodwind, piano, guitar, bass, drums and percussion, recruited a team of singers and awaited orders. He knew that he was going to have to produce eight to ten songs per show, and he knew that most of that music would be new arrangements of contemporary popular songs. The rest he had to work out as he went along.

'For that first series, I wrote every crotchet and quaver that was played,' he says. 'For three months I didn't leave my music room, I was just writing, writing, writing. I became a zombie, and the worst thing is, I enjoyed it and I got totally hooked on the deadlines. But, for the second series, I had to call in a bit of help – the series got longer, and there's only so much that one person can do.'

MAKING THE MUSIC

The process of turning pop songs into live dance music calls on a wide range of skills, and also takes full advantage of new technology. The songs are chosen by the production team, 'with a little bit of advice from me,' says Holloway, 'because at first they didn't understand basic things about tempo. They'd send me songs for waltzes that weren't in 3:4 time, and I'd have to explain that while I could work a lot of miracles, that was one that was beyond me.' The selections mixed classics ('The Lady is a Tramp', 'Let's Face the Music and Dance') with pop standards ('Roxanne', 'How Deep is Your Love') and more recent chart material ('Leave Right Now', 'Livin' La Vida Loca').

It's one thing for Holloway to rearrange the songs for his band ('That's the sort of thing I can pretty much do with my eyes closed'), but first the numbers have to be edited to fit the one-minute-30-second format of the routines. So the commercial tracks are emailed to studio wizard Graham Jarvis, who, in consultation with the dancers, picks out the highlights of a song and glues them together into a working track. 'I use software called Cubase SX,' says Jarvis. 'It's very good for cutting and pasting, but it also allows me to smooth out the tempos and add false endings where

necessary. Older songs tend to vary a lot in tempo – they speed up for the chorus or the final verse – and that's hard for the dancers. Also, a lot of commercial tracks fade at the end, and the dancers need a definite ending. I can sort all that out in the studio, and provide an edited track that they can rehearse to.'

Jarvis's edited version is then emailed to Laurie Holloway, who plays it on his computer and starts arranging. 'Computers are wonderful things,' he says, 'because they've cut out all that toing and froing we used to do. In the old days, I had to meet my music

copyist in a lay-by on the M4 to hand things over; now I just wait for it to drop into my mailbox. But when it comes to arranging, I do it with paper and pencil – it's what I'm used to, and it's faster.

'So I listen to Graham's track, then I go to the piano and work out the key. I mark up my scoresheets, then write down the intro and all the different band parts. I have to transpose some parts on to other instruments – I don't have strings in my band, for instance, so I might give the string part to flutes, or I can do them on my keyboard, a Yamaha Clavinova. The whole thing takes me about three hours, then I fax it all over to my music copyist who produces the band parts. It's a pretty slick operation now.'

While Holloway is busy with the arrangements, the dancers are rehearsing to Jarvis's edited studio track – so there can be an element of surprise when they first hear the live version. 'It shouldn't be too much of a shock,' says Holloway, 'because we observe strict tempo, and all the bits that they're used to will be there. Once or twice I've had dancers (naming no names), going off at me about how I ruined their chances by changing the music, but I check back and make sure that our arrangements are identical in all fundamental respects to what they've used. It sounds different – it's a live band – but it's the same piece.'

PLAYING IT LIVE

On the day of the show, the band has only an hour's rehearsal time for all its numbers, and 20 minutes of that is taken up with sound-checks. 'All we can do is run through our parts and make sure the numbers work. To all intents and purposes, the musicians are sight-reading. But that's not a problem, that's what they're trained to do – they're the best session musicians in the country. The A-team. And if any of them aren't available, there's another A-team. There is no such thing as a B-team.' After the band rehearsal (which the dancers often spy on, to get a sneak preview of the sound), there's a full dress run

– the first time that all the elements of the show come together. And then, show time.

'The best thing about *Strictly Come Dancing*,' says Holloway, 'is that it's live. There are no retakes. It's like old-fashioned light entertainment, but it has much more atmosphere. It takes me back to the days when I used to play for the *Rolf Harris Show*, or the *Val Doonican Show*. I like that big-band feel, and it's something new for me. I've even had to have music stands made for the band with my name on; you've got to have that, haven't you? Fortunately my trumpet player fronts the Bert Kaempfert band, so he knew someone who could make them for us.'

The success of *Strictly Come Dancing* has led to more big-band gigs for Holloway and his team – 'which is great, but a lot of hard work. I always had a trio before, and, believe me, that's a lot easier to manage.' He's also become firm friends with his presenter-in-chief. 'Bruce is a jazz piano player, too, so we have a bit of fun writing things together. He lives

In the spirit of Saturday-night live entertainment the programme's band often made way for some of the music industry's star talents to join in. Guest artists have included Donny Osmond, Westlife, Michelle Williams (from Destiny's Child) and Shania Twain.

just a few miles from my house, so it's easy to get together and play.'

When he's not putting the dancers through their paces, Holloway is at ITV providing music for Michael Parkinson's show. 'That runs from September too, so during the autumn I'm working flat out. Parkinson is two days a week; *Strictly Come Dancing* is five. It's great for my ego, but it's not doing a lot for my social life.'

And the secret of his success? 'I work fast,' says Holloway, 'and I don't make mistakes. But to be honest, I think the reason producers like me is because I turn up on time and I don't get drunk till after the show's over. You know what musicians can be like.'

Celebrities

Series Three

Zoe Ball

Zoe Ball claims to have 'hung up her raving shoes since becoming a mum'. The woman once known for clubbing until the wee small hours now restricts her dancing to weddings.

NAME Zoe Ball
DAY JOB Radio and TV presenter
DANCE PARTNER Ian Waite

'I love dancing with the dads and uncles at weddings, because they always know what they're doing and there's something great about being flung around by a man.'

There should be ample opportunity for being flung around in *Strictly Come Dancing*, if Ball can relocate her raving shoes. Being married to a DJ must help too. 'For my wedding dance Norman [alias Fatboy Slim] and I worked on a few moves, but we were so drunk we forgot to dance – and we even forgot to cut the cake. Later, at Kirsty Young's wedding, the same song came on quite by chance, so we finally got to do it just for each other.'

While presenting *Strictly Dance Fever* – before she had agreed to do *Strictly Come Dancing* – Ball had an embarrassing brush with dancing. 'I begged the producer to let me dance with one of the dancers at the start of the show. In rehearsals it was perfect – but once it came to the real thing I totally messed up and threw myself on the floor. It was a classic Bridget Jones moment, and I even revealed my knickers.'

Ball's favourite form of dancing is 'idiot dancing – which I do in the bathroom to amuse my son', but she's aware that her professional partner will require more discipline from her than that. 'He'll have to be strict and force me to concentrate. And I need to remember that if he tells me off I can't sulk! I want to get through the first few weeks so I can do the Tango, because I think the costumes are going to look so funny on me. I'm not very feminine, and my fear is that I might end up looking like a Tweenie, but the chance to do that dance would be great.'

Darren Gough

As a cricketer, Darren Gough has been described as dazzling, extrovert and inspiring. But will those qualities translate on to the dance floor?

Gough's the first to admit that his post-match dancing is usually alcohol-inspired, and that the last time he stepped out his partner was Freddie Flintoff. 'We did a few rock 'n' roll moves after a semi-final win against Australia. At least it was a bit better than the dancing I used to do when I was 18 or 19 – then I just jumped around like an idiot thinking I was cool. It was fun at the time, but it must have looked shocking. I worked up a few Elvis and Shakin' Stevens moves, and won a rock 'n' roll dancing competition – but then only three people entered.'

Gough's not short of energy and enthusiasm, but channelling those qualities into the highly disciplined world of ballroom dancing may not be easy. 'I'm a cheeky, jack-the-lad bloke, and I think most people would expect me to do something like *Celebrity Love Island* rather than *Strictly Come Dancing*. I'm the total opposite to what you'd expect as a ballroom dancer, and that's why it should be fun for the viewers to watch. As a sportsman I'm naturally competitive, but it remains to be seen if I'm a quick learner. I'll give 120 per cent, but I think I'm going to be rubbish. I hope my personality will win me votes – like Christopher Parker's did.'

Being an England cricket hero is probably enough in itself to propel Gough to the semi-finals at least; he's also confident that there will be a sufficient spark between him and his professional partner to keep the viewers interested. 'The prettier she is the better,' he says. 'Let's just hope she doesn't fall for me.'

NAME Darren Gough
DAY JOB Cricketer
DANCE PARTNER Lilia Kopylova

Siobhan Hayes

The My Family *star isn't going in to* Strictly Come Dancing *with a killer instinct. 'Everyone wants to win,' says Siobhan Hayes, 'but I'm just going to wait and see what happens.'*

NAME Siobhan Hayes
DAY JOB Actor, *My Family*
DANCE PARTNER Matthew Cutler

'Someone has to go out in the first week, and if it's me then so be it. Such is life.' This might not be the right frame of mind with which to enter the competitive arena of this live Saturday-night television series, but Hayes is remarkably laid back about the whole experience to come. 'I've always believed that it's good to learn a new skill, and what better skill to have than dancing? Maybe if I become a good enough dancer I might get a job in a musical. I recently went to see *The Producers* in the West End, and I was struck by how much fun everyone seemed to be having. I'd love to have a go at that.'

Hayes joined the popular and long-running sitcom *My Family* in its third series, playing Susan Harper's (Zoe Wanamaker) niece, Abi. 'I was temping when I got called to the audition. I didn't feel very hopeful about getting the part and I also didn't want to be left without a job, so I made an excuse to get out of work so that I could go to the audition. It went really well and so they called me back for a second reading. That time I was really nervous.' So if she gets through the first week, will Hayes be a nervous wreck on the dance floor? 'I'm going to take it one dance at a time and see how it goes. I'd like to get as far as doing the Waltz, because it's so ladylike and elegant. But even though it looks easy, I'm sure it's going to be really hard to learn.'

Colin Jackson

Athletes have always done well on Strictly Come Dancing; *they at least have the advantage of being physically fit, as Denise Lewis, Roger Black and Martin Offiah have proved.*

And if they have a sense of rhythm as well, they're guaranteed a place in the second half of the series. 'I like all sorts of music – anything with a good rhythm, basically – so that shouldn't be too much of a problem.' But Jackson's not naturally at home on the dance floor. 'I haven't danced since I was a kid. I used to dance around the room to *Top of the Pops*, and my mum and dad and uncle would pay me 5p for every song I'd dance to. Since then – nothing. I don't even dance in clubs; I'm frightened of getting creased!'

At least Jackson's not frightened of competition; since winning his first Olympic medal in 1988, he's broken records all over the world and still holds the world record for the indoor 60m Hurdles and the outdoor 110m Hurdles. Even more promisingly, he recently took part in a shark-baiting programme – and a man who's prepared to do that is presumably not afraid of Craig Revel Horwood, Arlene Phillips et al. 'I'm not scared of a challenge and I also see *Strictly Come Dancing* as an opportunity to learn a new skill.'

Having watched his friend and fellow Olympic athlete Denise Lewis glide her way into the series-two final, Jackson's got his eye on the prize. 'There's only one goal in this competition, and that's to win the final. It's the same as in athletics. I learned a lot from watching Denise last series, so I think I've got some idea of what's needed. The only thing that's worrying me is the idea of dancing so close to a complete stranger. That's going to feel really spooky at first.'

NAME Colin Jackson CBE
DAY JOB Olympic athlete and sports commentator
DANCE PARTNER Erin Boag

Gloria Hunniford

An old hand at live television and radio, Strictly Come Dancing should hold no fear for Gloria Hunniford.

In the course of a 40-year career, she's tackled most of the challenges that broadcasting and show business can throw at her, and she has always come out smiling. She's even danced in front of the most difficult audience of them all – the Royal Family. 'Esther Rantzen and I did a turn at the *Royal Variety Performance*,' she says. 'We rehearsed in a room no bigger than a broom cupboard, and then we were unleashed on to a massive stage. Our choreographer was in the wings shouting, "Turn! Turn! Turn!" as we sang "Anything You Can Do, I Can Do Better". Which, clearly, we couldn't!'

After that baptism of fire, Hunniford should be able to glide through *Strictly Come Dancing* with the confidence and ease that characterizes every aspect of her professional persona. But can a 65-year-old woman really hope to compete with the likes of Jaye Jacobs (23), or professional athlete Colin Jackson? 'I've seen how tough the training is,' she says, 'and I'm just hoping that the show will make me fitter! My only worry is that my feet won't do what my brain is telling them to. I was taught to dance as a child, so I've got an instinct for it, and I understand the fundamentals of ballroom dancing – that's where I think older contestants have an edge over the younger ones. As long as I don't fall down the stairs before I've even got on to the dance floor, I should be fine.'

NAME Gloria Hunniford
DAY JOB TV presenter
DANCE PARTNER Darren Bennett

James Martin

'I only really dance when I'm drunk,' says chef James Martin, 'and even then there's nothing good about it. The last time I danced was on a Friday night with my mates in the pub. There's always alcohol involved.'

This may not be a good omen for Martin's *Strictly Come Dancing* performance, as hiccuping and staggering won't impress the judges, but he's determined to prove himself. 'I want to succeed. I can guarantee that I'll try harder than anyone else; as a chef, I'm used to putting in the hours. I hope the judges and the public will notice my hard work, even if I'm not quite Fred Astaire.'

One thing he won't suffer from is stage fright: he's been performing on television regularly since 1996, and has played to packed houses across the UK in the *Ready Steady Cook* Roadshow. 'It's an unbelievable feeling to walk out to 2500 people who just want to watch you cook an omelette. Dancing must be like cooking to a recipe; you just need practice, practice, practice.'

Since signing up for the show, Martin has been hitting the gym in an attempt to improve his fitness before he goes in to the rigorous training programme. 'For a chef, the idea of a gym is like hell on earth, but I really hope that one thing I'm going to get out of doing the series is fitness. My worst fear is that I'll drop my partner, or fall over.'

So how does he reconcile his heart throb image (*Company* magazine voted him one of the UK's 50 most eligible bachelors) with swanning around a dance floor in rhinestones? 'In Yorkshire, where I grew up, men are supposed to be men. You can imagine how embarrassing it was to line up next to my friends, all in their rugby kits, while I was holding a cooking basket. If I'd danced as well as I cooked, my dad may have disowned me. But I enjoy a challenge.'

NAME James Martin
DAY JOB Chef
DANCE PARTNER Camilla Dallerup

Jaye Jacobs

Like most young actors, Jaye Jacobs has been well trained in the art of dance. She studied tap as a child in Bath, then went to London to take up a Dance and Drama course at the Arts Educational School.

So, on paper at least, it appears that she's a shoo-in for the series-three final, but she insists, 'I was never any good at dancing, though. When I was at college I was always bottom in the dance classes; it was acting and singing that I was good at. I was classified as "an actor who can move" – which means I was pretty useless at dancing. I love it, though. I'm always dancing to music in my head, even when I'm on the set at *Holby City*. And I love getting up to dance at the Notting Hill Carnival – when you can really let your hair down without caring what you look like.'

The discipline of ballroom dancing may come as a challenge to a woman who describes herself as 'hyperactive', but she's prepared to put in the hours – despite the fact that previous contestants from long-running series such as *Holby City* and *Casualty* have found it hard to balance the demands of two very hard jobs. 'I've done it before. When I was still at college, I got my first professional job in the West End production of *Rent*; for three months I was studying by day and performing at night. I didn't know whether I was coming or going – but it prepared me for most things.'

Now she's ready to plunge into a very different world: 'When else will it be acceptable to don sequins? I want to be daring with the costumes and the dancing and the music. My only big fear is that my boobs will pop out.'

NAME Jaye Jacobs
DAY JOB Actor, *Holby City*
DANCE PARTNER Andrew Cuerden

Dennis Taylor

Ladies, beware: Dennis Taylor is about to take to the dance floor. The former world-snooker champion, TV commentator, recording artist (number six in 1986 as guest vocalist on Chas & Dave's 'Snooker Loopy') and eyewear model could be the big surprise of the third series.

'I've been dancing ever since I was a boy growing up in Ireland. Back then all anyone did was play football and dance. All my aunts were good dancers, and one in particular was an amazing Irish dancer, so it's in my blood. In those days I could jive with two girls at once – which was very hard to do, and so anyone who could do that was looked up to.'

Taylor has been a fan of *Strictly Come Dancing* since it first began. 'I was an avid fan of the first two series, never missing an episode, and the challenge of seeing how good I could become alongside a professional dancer is an attractive one to me. I hope that the constant training will get me fitter, because the only exercise I get these days is walking around a golf course.'

During his snooker career, Taylor's wisecracking persona masked a determination to succeed. Never more so than in his epic title fight against Steve Davis in the 1985 World Snooker Championships – a match that was watched by a record TV audience of 18.5 million and a game that he won on the final black. 'I was so nervous during that final frame. Steve was looking whiter and whiter; I was looking redder and redder. People at home had to keep adjusting their colour controls.' But he's entering *Strictly Come Dancing* in a considerably more chilled frame of mind. 'I have no intention of winning the thing. My main focus is to have as much fun as possible, and see how good I can become under the wing of a professional dancer.'

NAME Dennis Taylor
DAY JOB World-snooker champion and commentator
DANCE PARTNER Izabela Hannah

Patsy Palmer

Patsy Palmer is more famous for her voice – which echoed around Albert Square for the six years that she played Bianca – than for her dancing.

NAME Patsy Palmer
DAY JOB Actor
DANCE PARTNER Anton du Beke

In her younger days, before her three children came along, she could be found dancing around her handbag with the best of them, but she never took it that seriously. 'I did dance classes when I was a kid,' she says, 'but I was always skipping them. My mum would drop me off at the dance school and as soon as she'd gone I'd go to the Wimpy across the road and spend my class money on a burger instead.'

Since leaving *EastEnders* in 1999, Palmer has had a stab at professional dancing, playing a tap teacher in the musical *Stepping Out*, for which she had to train hard. She's adamant that this doesn't give her an unfair advantage over other competitors, though. '*Stepping Out* was a big challenge because dance teachers need to look confident. But there were only a few set routines for that production – *Strictly Come Dancing* is going to be much harder because there are so many routines to learn. If there are any dancers as good as Jill Halfpenny in this series, then I don't stand a chance.'

So why has she agreed to compete? 'My mother-in-law said she wouldn't speak to me if I didn't! Her family are big fans of the show, and they can't wait to see me on it. Raising money for charity is also a huge motivation – and I can't wait to wear those gorgeous dresses. I also hope that all that dance training will help me tone up.' Palmer is a great believer in the beneficial effects of dance – in 2002, she released her own fitness video, which was based around dance moves.

Will Thorp

Previous experience suggests that trying to compete in Strictly Come Dancing *while holding down a day job in a long-running medical drama isn't easy – but* Casualty *star Will Thorp is determined to have a go.*

'Casualty is a six-day week,' says Thorp, who plays Paul 'Woody' Joyner in the show, 'and it can be gruelling. I can remember watching Sarah Manners [*Casualty*'s Bex, who competed in the second series] and thinking how stressful the live performance must be. In fact, whenever I've seen *Strictly Come Dancing*, I've always felt really sorry for the contestants. How ironic: that's now going to be me.'

Apart from a bit of training at drama school, Thorp has had minimal dance experience. 'Me and a mate used to re-create the lift from *Dirty Dancing*, and many's the time we were asked to leave a club after that one. The last time I danced was at my wedding two years ago. To say I'm rusty is generous: I'm totally seized up. My wife thinks it's ridiculous, but she can't wait to see me in action.'

Thorp's considerable *Casualty* following should carry him a long way (previous series have shown that good-looking young men can always rise above a lack of natural dance talent), but, beyond that, Thorp's relying on his partner to push him. 'I'm the first person to say I have absolutely no hopes of winning the programme, but I'm well up for it. I hope my partner is strict, and works me hard, because I prefer to put in the effort and not give up until I can do something. I'll work hard for her if she makes me, even if I am tired. I'm particularly looking forward to the Latin dances – I think the sexy moves will be fun!'

NAME Will Thorp
DAY JOB Actor, *Casualty*
DANCE PARTNER Hanna Haarala

Fiona Phillips

If one breakfast-television presenter can do it, then why not another? Fiona Phillips must be hoping that the GMTV audience have taken her to their hearts in sufficient numbers to send her in Natasha Kaplinsky's footsteps all the way to the series crown.

NAME Fiona Phillips
DAY JOB *GMTV* presenter
DANCE PARTNER Brendan Cole

And, like Kaplinsky, Phillips was initially reluctant to take the challenge. 'I don't know why I agreed to this. My agent put a lot of pressure on me. I kept saying, "No, no, and no again!" Eventually, it was my husband who convinced me; once I had his support, I knew I could do it.'

Phillips has been reporting for *GMTV* since 1993, when she made her début covering the Los Angeles earthquake. 'I was an entertainment correspondent in LA – and I woke up one morning to find the room shaking and things crashing down. I raced into work and the road was literally splitting apart around me.' Since that unsettling start, she's covered numerous big Hollywood stories like the O.J. Simpson and Michael Jackson cases, before coming back to Britain and the relative safety of the *GMTV* red sofa.

Getting up early, dealing with earthquakes or murders is all in a day's work – but dancing definitely isn't. 'I actively dislike dancing. When I'm out with friends and they say, "Let's dance", I pretend to go to the loo. At school discos I just stood in a circle and swayed to the songs.'

Now she's hoping that her partner can carry her some of the way to success. 'I'll be better at the dances where I can cling on to someone, like in the Waltz. It'll be awful when I'm left to do something on my own. If I'd lived in Jane Austen's time I might have been ok: the stately dances appeal to me much more than jigging about on the dance floor.'

Bill Turnbull

Could BBC Breakfast News *have another secret dance champion on its hands? Bill Turnbull has been grilling colleague Natasha Kaplinsky for dance tips ever since signing up to the third series of* Strictly Come Dancing.

'I have followed the show ever since the beginning, because Natasha was involved. I know she'll be a flag-bearer for me, and I'm very encouraged by the last series because there were people in there who were as rhythmically challenged as me.'

But middle-aged men haven't always fared well on the show, as David Dickinson and Quentin Willson can testify. However, although Turnbull has no pretensions to being a natural dancer, he does have the considerable advantage of being physically fit. In 2005, he completed his fifth London marathon, running the entire course dressed in a beekeeper's outfit (he's a keen apiculturist) in just over four and a half hours. 'But I'm not a natural dancer, much to my wife's irritation. She says that if I could create a sitting-down-with-a-beer dance, that would be my favourite. The last time I actually danced was in a sports store with my children. They were playing some rap music, and I started body popping. The kids were mortified.'

After an even more embarrassing display on *Children in Need* in 2004, when Turnbull actually fell on his backside during the dress rehearsal, he's developed a strategy for *Strictly Come Dancing*. 'If I can get through the first round, then I'll take it week by week and just try not to embarrass myself or my family too much. I need to leave the competition knowing how to do at least one dance properly – because then I'll have no more excuse not to dance with my wife at parties.'

NAME Bill Turnbull
DAY JOB News journalist, BBC *Breakfast News* presenter
DANCE PARTNER Karen Hardy

Andrew Cuerden

Another of the many talented dancers to come from southern Africa to compete in the UK, Andrew Cuerden grew up in Zimbabwe and took his first tentative steps on to the dance floor at his older sister's 21st birthday party.

'I was eight years old, painfully shy and self-conscious, and wild horses could not have pulled me on to a dance floor. But my sister, the party animal of the family, dragged me on kicking and screaming and gave me my first informal dance lesson. I then asked everyone at the party to dance and didn't stop until four in the morning.' Cuerden took up dance lessons in his teens, alternating it with rugby matches at the weekends. 'My girlfriends from dancing used to come and support me at rugby, so my team mates soon got jealous that I was getting the babes and they weren't!' Eventually, he had to make a choice between his two favourite pastimes, and he opted to pursue dancing, competing for seven years in South Africa before moving to England in the mid-90s. 'My dance teacher used to get friends in England to record *Come Dancing*, and we got all our choreographic ideas from those tapes. We used to look forward to professional couples coming over from England to demonstrate and teach. That's what made me decide to come to England and train.'

Cuerden's amateur career culminated with reaching fourth place in the English rankings, before turning professional in 2005 with his dance partner, Hanna Haarala. Now he's looking forward to putting his celebrity partner Jaye Jacobs through her paces. 'Celebrities are just people; they're beginners – and I'm used to dealing with beginners on a daily basis. The only difference will be that there's a camera in the room. The essential ingredient to a successful partnership is mutual respect – obviously, I'll respect her for who she is and what she has done to get where she has, but I shall also expect that she respects that I am serious about my career. And I'll do my very best to make us both look and feel fantastic.'

Hanna Haarala

Hanna Haarala was unwilling to get too involved with dancing in her childhood: she was already a keen ice-skater, and that's where she saw her future. 'At my first dance class at the age of ten, I said, "I will not stop ice-skating because of dancing." Three months later, that's exactly what I did.'

Throughout her teens in her native Finland, Haarala worked her way through the competitive circuit and started teaching as well. With her partner, Mikko Kaasalainen, she represented Finland at the European and World Games, before dissolving the partnership after three years. That's when Andrew Cuerden stepped in, calling her up with a view to a try-out and flying to Finland to meet her. 'I liked his personality and I thought it would be good for me to move to London and learn more about dancing. It all happened really quickly. He flew to Finland for a trial, I flew to London for a trial and we decided after one lesson to form a partnership.' The Haarala–Cuerden partnership doesn't extend beyond the dance floor, though; she has a boyfriend, Joe, tucked away at home.

The prospect of teaching celebrities in *Strictly Come Dancing* doesn't phase Haarala at all, largely because she's blissfully unaware of who most of them are. 'I don't know any English celebrities!' she says. 'I hope my partner won't be offended, because I won't know who he is. I just hope he's not too tall – I'm only 5ft 2in, and it will be difficult to dance with him if he's very big.' And when the competition gets going, the gloves will be off. 'I am very competitive. If both Andrew and I got to the final, I would wish him the best of luck but deep down I would want to beat him and win.'

Izabela Hannah

Like many a young girl before her, Izabela Hannah was lured into dance classes by seeing Patrick Swayze in Dirty Dancing *at an impressionable age.*

'After I saw the wonderful dancing in that film, I made my parents take me to dance school,' she says. 'I learned everything from disco to Rumba. It was easy for me to commit to dance, because I loved it so much.'

From there, Hannah worked her way through the ranks of the competitive circuit at home in Poland, where she became Amateur Ballroom Champion in 2001 and 2002. After that she moved to America, where she met her teacher Stephen Hannah. At first the relationship was professional – he was helping her to find a new dance partner – but when she accompanied him to Britain, a romance began and they married in 2003. Stephen Hannah is a former British Open Champion, but retired from competition in 2000. 'I practise two hours every day with Stephen, and if he would come out of retirement we could beat anyone, even Anton du Beke and Erin Boag!'

The key to Hannah's teaching method (and she hopes this will rub off on her celebrity partner Dennis Taylor) is 'passion and excitement. That's what I've always felt when I dance, and when people come to my studio for classes they say that's what I give them. Hopefully, that will happen with Dennis. I am a very passionate person, and I know I can use that to push him a little bit further. I just hope I get enthusiasm and commitment in return.'

Matthew Cutler

Of all the new dancers to appear in the third series of Strictly Come Dancing, Matthew Cutler should have the biggest advantage: his former wife and professional partner, Nicole Cutler, appeared in series two.

However, there's no whiff of nepotism here: Mr Cutler won the British and UK Closed Professional Latin Championships last year, and the World and European Championships this year, as well as gaining a whole cupboard full of other trophies since he started dancing at the age of ten. The Cutlers split in 2003; he now dances with Danish champion, Charlotte Engstrand.

He describes his dance style as 'sensual and sexy. I don't like the gymnastic style where the priority is trick steps and things like that. I can really get into the Jive, as it's a relaxed dance and not very controlled and restricted.' But will he be able to relax with a celebrity in his arms – possibly one who isn't a natural dancer? 'I don't really mind who I teach as long as she is willing to learn and not worried about making a fool of herself. It's so draining when you're trying to teach someone and they don't really want to learn.'

And how does he feel about taking on fellow professionals and rivals like Darren Bennett and Anton du Beke? 'I'm quite competitive, and I hate to lose. I'd rather not take part in something if I knew that I wasn't going to have a good chance of winning, whether it's tennis, or running, or stupid things like arm-wrestling in the pub.'

Karen Hardy

In Latin-American circles, the name of Karen Hardy is spoken with reverence. With her professional partner Bryan Watson – a former World, International, European, United Kingdom and British Amateur Latin Champion – she was at the very top of the profession throughout the 90s.

Hardy was already a very experienced competitive dancer – but Watson was 'a god. In every form of art or sport, there's someone who comes along and is a phenomenon – a Tiger Woods or a Rudolf Nureyev. Bryan was one of these.' During their five-year partnership they represented England all over the world, and became one of the most respected partnerships. She retired in 1999, but not before they had been credited with breaking the mould of Latin-American dancing, and dragging the dance form into the 21st century. 'To create a step and then see it copied around the world is an indescribable reward. They don't come any more dedicated and focused than Bryan, and that's why we were able to break the rules that had been set in stone for so long.'

Now, Hardy faces yet another challenge – getting back into shape after being away from competitive dancing for six years. Most recently she's been teaching, as well as being a sought-after judge – and she's just had a son, Callum. 'I train my students to perform at the highest standard, so now I have to put my money where my mouth is. Callum is only six months old, and to be honest the last thing in the world I feel like doing is hitting the gym. It hurts like mad, but all I can think about is walking onto that floor again. I thought that once the midnight bell had chimed, that was it for Cinderella. I didn't think a Prince Charming would come looking for me or that I'd ever get the chance to wear the dresses again. The hardest thing will be putting the heels back on: it's been five years since I've moved in a pair of three-inch heels, and that in itself is going to be crippling!'

The Dances

Rumba

From Africa, via Cuba to America, the Rumba is the number that burns up the dance floor with an irresistible mixture of sexual passion and rhythm

The Rumba is a romantic dance; it tells the story of seduction between a man and a woman. They flirt, then there's attraction. The woman then tries to get away, but the man pulls her back. It's the only slow Latin-American dance – and rhythm is all. The couple has to be connected, disciplined and always showing the right kind of lines. It's one of the hardest dances for a beginner to master – but in the hands of the professionals, the Rumba is one of the sexiest performances on the dance floor. Here Darren Bennett and Lilia Kopylova demonstrate the classic Rumba positions.

History

The rumba has always had a slightly risqué reputation in dance circles. Its origins are ancient, going back to African ritual dances that were transported to the New World by the slave trade. It surfaced in its modern form in Cuba in the 1890s, when it was repressed by the authorities for its 'lewdness' and overt sexual overtones. A sanitised version was popularised in America in the 1930s, where it spread rapidly due to the popularity of songs such as 'The Peanut Vendor'. It retains core elements of sexual teasing and female domination; essentially, it's a dance of seduction.

Make-up. Like all Latin dances, skin and hair tones tend to be dark, with smoky eyes for the women. Lilia's hair is worn up, in a style that evokes the nightclubs of the 1930s and 40s.

Dress. A simple black silhouette for Darren, to accentuate the line of the dance. Women's Rumba dresses are often cut away and revealing, to accentuate the sexual nature of the dance of seduction.

Posture. The Rumba is all based around the classic Latin-American hold but, as it progresses, the dancers' bodies will be alternately erect and sinuous.

Feet. Feet remain toned at all times throughout the Rumba. Although it's a slow dance, the dancers must maintain a disciplined line that 'follows through' the extremities.

Close Hold
The standard Latin-American hold, just before going into the dance. The points of contact are his right arm with her left, and opposite hands. Bodies are toned, and there's a clear connection between the couple.

Arms. In ballroom, there's full body contact between the dancers, making it easier for the man to lead. In Latin dances it's all through the hands – so arms must be strong and toned to carry the message.

Legs. Shifting weight from one leg to the other thrusts the hips from side to side – much more subtle than a bum-wiggle. The resting leg is extended to accentuate the line.

Len Says...

What we're looking for in the Rumba is a connection between the couple. When Darren and Lilia dance the Rumba, they're looking at each other nearly all the time – and you can see the connection through their arms and hands, the slightest pressure and she's spinning round. It's all about that contact. Look at the basic hold, and you'll see that, although they're barely touching, they're still communicating. The Rumba should be romantic rather than sexy; it's all about seduction and courtship. The man might be leading, but if you look at the basic hold you see that in the Rumba, as in life, the girl always has the upper hand.

⬅ Fan Position
A basic Rumba step, showing how the man leads through the simplest of hand connections. The couple step apart, finishing at right angles to one another.

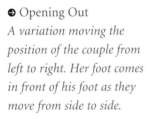

➡ Opening Out
A variation moving the position of the couple from left to right. Her foot comes in front of his foot as they move from side to side.

⬆ Sliding Doors
An advanced version of a basic Rumba step. The line is almost symmetrical – but he's on his forward foot, she's on the back foot. The couple will then cross positions to the other side.

 Rope Spin

The man supports the woman with his right arm while she spins on the balls of her feet and turns. The feet are crossed, one in front of the other, before she whips round in a spiral move.

 Romance

A typical Rumba pose or 'line', showing the romance of the dance, with the woman's head resting on the man's chest, his hand caressing her neck. Despite the mood, limbs remain toned at all times.

 Rumba Drop

One of the most spectacular moments in the Rumba, and a guaranteed crowd-pleaser. Despite the abandon of the pose, the line remains correct from the tips of fingers to the end of toes.

Rumba Line

Sometimes the Rumba can get pretty athletic. In this typical rumba line the man holds the woman by hooking her leg around his waist.

Who Did Well...

Natasha Kaplinsky performed the highest-scoring rumba in the first series (36 out of 40), but there still wasn't quite enough 'basic' – fan positions and opening outs – for Len Goodman's taste. **Jill Halfpenny** and **Denise Lewis** both scored 32 in the second series – proving that the rumba is one of the hardest dances to master, even for the champions. For the less naturally gifted dancers, it's a Latin nightmare: **Christopher Parker** and **Esther Rantzen** only scraped 16 points. But when you look at the discipline, technique and athleticism that's required, that suddenly doesn't seem like quite such a shoddy score.

Waltz

The epitome of elegance, the Waltz is the dance that most people think characterizes ballroom dancing. But the shuffling of amateurs demonstrates that it is more complicated than it appears.

The Waltz, of course, is danced in 3:4 time – hence the rhythmical rise and fall of the movement that's made it a ballroom favourite for 200 years. The communication between the couple is so intense in the Waltz that they should move almost as one, never breaking the contact that forms the classic ballroom hold. It's that high degree of touching that made the Waltz such a controversial dance in Victorian England, and which means it's still one of the most popular social dances in the world. Anton du Beke and Erin Boag demonstrate a dance that looks simple when it is done properly, but in reality is anything but…

History

Nowadays it's the epitome of elegant, old-fashioned ballroom dancing, but time was when the Waltz was regarded as scandalous and overtly sexual. Derived from the *volta*, a French peasant dance, it became popular in Vienna in the 18th century, spreading rapidly across Europe. When it reached England, it was immediately denounced in polite society for its excessive physical contact (social dances had hitherto kept partners at a decent arm's length). When the Prince Regent included it in a ball he held in 1816, *The Times* described the Waltz as 'the indecent foreign dance … an obscene display. We feel it a duty to warn every parent against exposing his daughter to so fatal a contagion.' Needless to say, it rapidly caught on.

Throwaway Oversway
A classic Waltz line. The man dances the woman round in front of him (small picture, left) before turning her and allowing her torso to extend back (main picture).

Make-up. The overall look for ballroom dances is less dramatic than the Latin section however, it is more elegant. In this photo Erin wears her hair loose for a free, flowing look (although it took hours to sew in the hair extensions) and her make-up is simple and natural.

Dress. Classic white tie and tails for the man, of course: that's the uniform for nearly all ballroom. The woman wears a light and floating dress that moves with her and accentuates her rhythm.

Arms. The arms must be kept in the correct ballroom hold (see next page) whatever position the dancers adopt.

Feet. The dancers rise and fall throughout the Waltz by coming up on to the balls of their feet, turning and stepping in the classic one-two-three rhythm of the music.

Legs. Symmetry is important, and so the positions of the partners' legs frequently mirror each other. The supporting leg, concealed by the elegance of the movement, is rock solid.

Posture. No matter what variations the dancers perform, the basic hold remains solid throughout the dance.

Len Says...

A Waltz should flow. It has a rise and fall, a lyrical, musical feeling that should be magical to watch. To an audience, it appears to float on a cloud – but the judges are looking for the strictest technique. It's all in that basic ballroom hold: his posture must be erect and vertical, and whatever shapes the couple get into they must maintain all the points of contact. But they're touching, not clinging – there should always be a lightness about it. The Waltz looks so easy, but in reality it's controlled chaos. You have to be very strong and supple to do all those turns and oversways, but the discipline is hidden by the magic and romance of the movement. It's an illusion.

⊘ ⊙ Ballroom Hold *(left and below) The dancers are not square on; the woman is slightly to the man's right. He places his right hand on the woman's back near the shoulder blade; her left hand rests on his right upper arm.*

⊘ Whisk
The dancers' feet end in a crossed position and the bodies and heads are in a position known as promenade position.

Natural Turn

'Natural' indicates a movement going to the right ('reverse' is to the left), commencing with the man's right foot. Body contact remains constant throughout, with no space between the hips.

Left Whisk

The man remains cool and controlled while the woman is turned through the full range of the whisk movement. Again, the strength of the supporting legs is concealed by the elegance of the turn.

Promenade

A basic forward ballroom movement. The couple moves around the floor while maintaining the all-important body contact.

Eros Line

Erin's up on the balls of her feet and Anton turns her into this elegant ballroom line where her position evokes the statue of Eros in Piccadilly Circus.

Who Did Well...

Considering it is a step that is so fundamental to ballroom dancing, the Waltz has always proved to be one of the hardest dances for the *Strictly Come Dancing* contestants to master. In fact, only two couples out of the first two series have managed to score over 30. **Natasha and Brendan** waltzed their way to an impressive 37 out of 40 in the semi-final of the first series, by which point they were both dancing like professionals. **Denise and Ian** had the unenviable challenge of making their series-two début with a Waltz – but they still managed a very creditable 31 points.

Paso Doble

In the ultimate expression of machismo, in this Spanish dance the man plays the role of the fearless matador, while the woman plays the cape and every other supporting role...

The melodramatic Paso Doble is one of the biggest challenges to the *Strictly Come Dancing* contestants. It's a deadly serious dance, charged with passion and violence – but, if it goes wrong, it can turn into low comedy. Even Lesley Garrett described it as 'a very silly dance', and images of Christopher Parker's bizarre interpretation of the Paso Doble are still burned on the memory. So how do the experts manage to make it work? Darren and Lilia, who are probably the best in the business, put the would-be bullfighters through their paces.

History

Unlike the rest of the Latin dances, the Paso Doble does not have its roots in Africa; this one comes directly from Spain. It's a stylized representation of the bullfight, with the man playing the part of the macho matador, the woman variously standing in for the bull, the cape, another matador or a dancer. **The dance (*paso doble* means 'two step') is based on the march music at the beginning of the *corrida*, progressing to the passes between bull and fighter, and moving towards the kill. This most dramatic and narrative of dances first became popular outside Spain during the 1930s, when it swept France and ultimately the entire ballroom-dancing world.**

Make-up. The Paso Doble must evoke the *corrida*, and so anything that adds to the Spanish vibe is useful. Black and red are the favoured colours – so Lilia favours dark eyes and dark lips, and accentuates her black curls with a huge red flower.

Arms. Arms and hands are constantly toned and flexed in the Paso Doble, emphasising the strength of the man and the suppleness of the woman. The flamenco feel extends through to the tips of the fingers.

Legs. A high degree of flexibility is necessary to carry off the Paso Doble properly. Both partners have to bend into extreme stretches, requiring a full range of mobility in their quadriceps and hamstrings.

Feet. The feet are used as a storytelling device in the Paso Doble: they are used to attract the bull's attention. As in all Latin dances, they remain strong and toned throughout.

⊘ Male Dominance
The man acts the part of the bullfighter in the Paso Doble, and all of his moves should accentuate his mastery of the situation. The woman is mostly the bullfighter's cape – as in this posture – bowing backwards.

Dress. Again, the mood is theatrically Spanish. Darren wears a stylized version of a bullfighter's bolero, black trimmed in red, while Lilia picks up the same colours in a flamenco-styled outfit with a tight bodice and full skirt.

Posture. Dramatic, exaggerated movements in the Paso Doble are accentuated by toned bodies flexing through the spine.

It's all about the focus and faces. You have to take this dance seriously and do it with commitment, otherwise it's not worth bothering. I look for good posture from the man, toned to the tips of his fingers, and for big dramatic shapes from the woman. They have to keep tight control in the basic steps, but go for the big effect in the attitudes (the lines they create). And they must look the part. It's no good going into a Paso Doble with a big smile. I want to see them looking angry – aggressive even. The eyes should always be focused, either on each other, on a judge, or even on a member of the audience. They must maintain that intensity right through the dance.

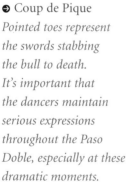

◔ Chassé Cape

On the third beat of the bar, the man passes the woman rapidly in front of him – imitating the bullfighter passing the cape as the bull charges past. A strong hold is essential to keep balance.

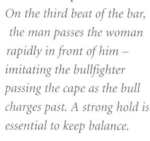

◔ Coup de Pique

Pointed toes represent the swords stabbing the bull to death. It's important that the dancers maintain serious expressions throughout the Paso Doble, especially at these dramatic moments.

◔ Matador Throws Cape

A typical Paso Doble line. The bullfighter tosses the cape disdainfully to the ground. Lilia uses her skirt to represent the cape's cloth, while Darren maintains the severe, erect line of the bullfighter.

⊖ Role Reversal

Sometimes the bull gets the upper hand – but the bullfighter shows his mastery of the situation by dropping down to demonstrate that he isn't impressed.

⊖ Elevations

A bit of all-important basic in the Paso Doble. Elevations are a series of small side steps, up on the balls of the feet – the bodies arch and the faces look down towards the floor.

⊗ Twist Turn

Once again, the woman is the cape being worked by the bullfighter. He puts his weight on his back leg, then she comes around in front of him and they turn on the balls of their feet.

⊖ Flamenco Checks

A typical flamenco move that's been incorporated into the Paso Doble. The couple dance in front of each other in a series of flexed leg movements going from right to left, working up an intensity as the moves continue.

Who Did Well...

For some of the couples, the paso doble was one dance too far; they couldn't master the steps or the attitude. But it also brought out some of the best performances of the whole show. **Jill and Darren** scored 37 in the second series semi-final, with **Denise and Ian** only one point behind them. **Natasha and Brendan** were the best Paso dancers in the first series, scoring 35 out of 40. But for many viewers, the abiding image of the Paso Doble event is **Christopher Parker** running around the dance floor trailing his cape like Superman. He only scored 15, but it was entertainment gold, and ensured his place in the semi-final.

Foxtrot

The Foxtrot is the most elegant and graceful of ballroom dances, which evokes images of Fred Astaire and Ginger Rogers and the ballroom dance floors of the 1930s.

The slow Foxtrot is every ballroom professional's favourite dance – an elegant, gliding, sophisticated number. As in all ballroom dances, however, complex technique is masked with an illusion of ease and grace (not least for the woman, who, in the immortal words of Ginger, has to do everything the man does but 'backwards and in heels'). It's founded on the basic ballroom hold (see p.120), around which is built a routine of turns and lines, the timing varying between slow and fast. At its simplest, the Foxtrot is a combination of walks and chassés, but in the hands of Anton and Erin it is a dazzling display of technique.

History

Back in 1914, at the height of the ragtime craze, American vaudeville performer Harry Fox was having difficulty finding women to partner him in a complicated two-step routine. As a result, he added slower steps, creating the slow-slow-quick-quick rhythm that that dance has today – and people started copying him. Before long, revellers at the *Jardin de Danse* nightclub – situated above the theatre where Fox was performing – started doing their own versions of 'Fox's Trot'. It was picked up by dance stars Vernon and Irene Castle, who incorporated it into their act and made it the epitome of ballroom grace and style that it remained through countless Astaire–Rogers films.

◔ Oversway into Aerial Ronde
The man holds the woman in the classic ballroom oversway (see p.119, and small picture, left) before turning her quickly in front of him. She finishes with one leg raised, hence 'aerial'.

Make-up. Think Hollywood, think understated glamour, think 1930s nightclubs, and you've got an idea of the Foxtrot style.

Arms. The classic ballroom hold leads the dancers through every permutation of the Foxtrot, allowing the man to communicate perfectly through his arms and hands with his partner.

Legs. In the simple version, the legs are more or less just stepping the couple around the floor. But as the Foxtrot becomes more complicated, the legs have to be precisely placed in order to achieve accurate turns.

Dress. As with the Waltz, the dress is elegant and flowing and the man is in ballroom tails.

Posture. A loose, carefree feel is essential to the Foxtrot, with the partners mirroring each other's movements as they spin and glide across the floor.

Feet. The Foxtrot requires the dancers to shift constantly from the ball to the heel of the foot – turning on the balls and pivoting on the heels. One of the hardest ballroom techniques.

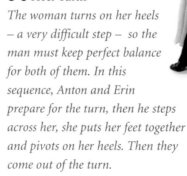

◔ Feather Step
The feather step – so-called because of the gentle curving shape formed by the foot – is a basic step of the Foxtrot. The man steps outside the woman on her right side on steps two and three.

◔ ◔ Heel Turns
The woman turns on her heels – a very difficult step – so the man must keep perfect balance for both of them. In this sequence, Anton and Erin prepare for the turn, then he steps across her, she puts her feet together and pivots on her heels. Then they come out of the turn.

⬅ Fallaway
*His left leg is back,
her right leg is
forward, and they
allow their upper bodies
to fall away from
each other while
maintaining the
correct ballroom
body contact
throughout.*

⬇ Same-foot Lunge
*A perfect example of how the couple's legs
mirror each other through the Foxtrot –
they both take their weight on to the
same leg. Anton holds Erin in an
oversway while their feet point out in the
same direction, extending the line.*

➋ Hover Cross
*Another bit of basic. The man steps
outside the woman on her left side,
and maintains body contact.*

Who Did Well...

Not surprisingly, this deceptively diffcult dance was a big challenge for the less gifted hoofers. **Natasha and Brendan** got the top mark in the first series – 35 out of 40 – but they were only a single point ahead of **Lesley and Anton**, who showed real aptitude for the gliding, free-and-easy style (and so they should; it's one of Anton's best dances). In the second series, only the eventual winners **Jill and Darren** could approach that standard, gaining 34 out of 40 points.

Jive

The closest thing to 'modern' dances on the night club dance floor, the Jive's origins are many and varied, making this a lively, fast and contemporary form of ballroom dancing.

It couldn't be further from the passion of the Paso Doble or the romance of the Rumba. The Jive is the light, bright, contemporary dance in the Latin-American canon, and it gives the dancers a chance to show off a much wider variety of moves, drawn from dozens of different traditions. The Jive may have solidified in the 40s and 50s with elements of the lindy hop and the jitterbug, but it continues to develop with greater freedom than any other dance. It's closer in nature to the social dancing that we're used to today – which might explain why some contestants felt they could take liberties with it that the judges didn't like!

History

The exact origins of the Jive are obscure: some say it's based on Seminole Indian dances, others that it derives, like so many Latin dances, from steps performed by African slaves in the New World. By the 1880s, a form of Jive was danced competitively in the southern states of the USA – but it wasn't until the jazz-crazed 1920s that the Jive became the official youth dance of America. With its quick movements and spins, it was frowned on by older, more traditional dancers. GIs brought the Jive to Europe in the 40s, where it was considered a 'corrupting influence' (just like the Waltz, over 100 years earlier). During the 50s, it mutated into swing, boogie-woogie, jitterbugging and rock and roll.

Make-up. The Jive is an informal party dance, and so the hair and make-up should give a celebratory, slightly cheeky feel. Lilia's hair is up loosely on one side – but it has to be sufficiently set so it won't whip around her face too much.

Dress. The Jive wardrobe 's eclectic roots. Darren's wearing a 50s-style purple jacket – very rock 'n' roll – while Lilia's matching dress is redolent of the 1920s and 30s with its bead fringing.

Feet. Fancy footwork is the name of the game in the Jive. The feet turn outwards into the chicken walk – or flick from the ankle – but all movements should be precise and completed.

◑ Hitch

A typical Jive move, showing the cheeky, celebratory nature of the dance. Arms extend in perfect lines front and back, while strong, precise leg movements provide lateral symmetry.

Arms. Arms are loose and expressive (although they shouldn't just be waved around any-old-how, as some contestants have tried). Postures and lines extend right through to the fingers.

Legs. Kicks from the hip, and flicks from the knee, make up many of the Jive's basic movements. The leg positions are often symmetrical, as here.

Posture. Far less rigid and erect than in other Latin dances, the body posture in the Jive must adapt to any of the athletic moves incorporated into the routine.

Len Says...

The Jive should be a bright and lively dance, a mixture of many different styles, so we're always looking for inventive choreography. But, you have to have technique as well, otherwise you end up like some of the contestants on the show, just running around the floor waving their hands in the air and doing no footwork at all. Jive can look like its pretty free-form at times, but in fact it's a stylized dance that takes elements from all over the place, and you'd better get them right or it's going to be a mess.

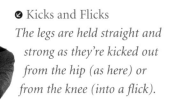

⊘ Kicks and Flicks
The legs are held straight and strong as they're kicked out from the hip (as here) or from the knee (into a flick).

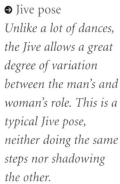

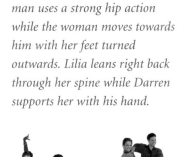

➔ Jive pose
Unlike a lot of dances, the Jive allows a great degree of variation between the man's and woman's role. This is a typical Jive pose, neither doing the same steps nor shadowing the other.

⬆ Chicken Walks
A basic Jive step, in which the man uses a strong hip action while the woman moves towards him with her feet turned outwards. Lilia leans right back through her spine while Darren supports her with his hand.

⊖ Jump On

This is a typical rock'n'roll move that's often incorporated into Jive performances – but it would not be allowed in competition, when the woman's feet must not both leave the ground.

➡ Jive Pivots

A continuous circling movement as the dancers turn round and round with a variety of arm positions throughout.

⊕ Stop-and-Go

The woman comes from the man's left, he stops her and returns her, making a yo-yo movement that's familiar on rock'n'roll dance floors.

⊖ Back Rock

This is the basic Jive step – the first thing you would learn if you went to Jive classes. Transferring the weight on to the back foot in small, quick movements allows for a full variety of turns.

Who Did Well...

Jill and Darren became the first couple ever to score a perfect 40 for their Jive on *Strictly Come Dancing*. They scored it in the final of the second series, and it was a marked improvement on their earlier attempt in the third week, when they scored 35. But that was still a long way ahead of any other Jive score in either series. **Aled** managed 32, but in the first series nobody got above **Lesley and Anton's** creditable 29.

Tango

Despite the salubrious origins of the dance, the aggressive yet sexy Tango is full of Latin passion and stirs up real excitement when danced with the control and power it demands.

The Tango brings a touch of Latin passion into the ballroom world – and it's a much more serious business than the frothy Foxtrot or the whirling Waltz. The lines are more rigid and severe and the movement staccato; it is more stop-and-go than the fluid sequences that are better known to ballroom dancers. Slow deliberate 'stalking' walks are alternated with sudden, fast action, which gives the dance its light and shade. It's been a tough nut to crack for the contestants on *Strictly Come Dancing*; if you don't have a natural sense of rhythm, you're never going to get the hang of the Tango.

History

Emerging from the black ghettos of Argentina in the 1890s, the Tango originated as a dance enacting the relationship between a prostitute and her client or between an unwilling woman and a smelly gaucho. The man's flexed-knee posture recalls the stiff-legged walk of the gauchos in their leather chaps; the woman's stance, head held back, allegedly derives from the fact that most of the men hadn't washed after a day on the range. In the prostitute and client story, her right hand, low in his hip, is supposed to be fishing for his wallet. Argentinian bands and dancers took the Tango to Europe in the 20th century, where it was cleaned up and became a pre-War craze – although it never lost its shady reputation.

Make-up. The Tango is the most severe of all the dances, so hair tends to be scraped back off the women's faces, aiming for a high-gloss, painted-on look. The make up is stark and dramatic.

⊘ Contra-check
A perfect expression of the passionate nature of the Tango. The man dominates the woman, leading her to lean away from him with her head and shoulders. She maintains a strong spine and firm arms.

Dress. Anton has changed his usual tails for something a little more loungey – a shorter jacket that reminds us of the Tango's informal roots. Erin completes her look with dramatic black and silver satin.

Arms. The arms are not so outstretched as in other ballroom dances and the man holds his partner closer to him, allowing the man to whisk the woman very quickly into dramatic positions.

Legs. The knees are slightly flexed throughout the Tango, so there is no rise and fall in this dance. Perfect leg control is necessary to produce the tense, stalking style that characterizes the dance.

Feet. In the Tango, the feet perform a lot of different moves – they drag across the floor, they flash and stab out into the air, they fly around in fast-paced changes or cruise through slow stalks.

Posture. The feel of the Tango is angular and sharp, so body shapes reflect that in a mixture of rigid stances. The dancers frequently hold each other at an estranging distance.

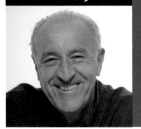

Len Says...

The Tango is an aggressive dance. There's not much smiling, but there's a lot of sex. At its best, the man should look like a raunchy gigolo who's quite capable of bending the woman over a table. Don't forget that it has its roots in a dance performed by Argentinian gauchos and prostitutes. While the Waltz and the Foxtrot are gliding dances, the Tango is flat and staccato, with sharp foot and head movements performed at lightning speed. Most dances are soft and rhythmic, but the Tango is very different and goes in big blips, like a heart monitor on a screen. It can be ugly if you do it badly, but done properly it's tremendously exciting.

Tango Hold

This differs from the basic ballroom hold. It's much tighter, his right arm is further round her body, and his left arm is closer to his body, pulling her inwards. Her left hand is further down, underneath his armpit.

Link

In the first step of the link (above left) Erin's head is to the left in a closed promenade position. Then they dance the link into the promenade position, before suddenly whipping her around (above right) back to a closed position again.

➲ Stalking Walks
Elongated steps commenced on the outside edge of the foot take the dancers across the floor. The taut attitude of the bodies and the stern facial expressions are an important part of the Tango.

⬆ Spanish Drag
The woman starts in a deep line, as the man slowly brings her up, then a little further up, before suddenly they both drop and turn into promenade position to continue their progress across the floor.

⬅ Swivel
There are many swivelling moves in the Tango, as the dancers turn on their feet and bring the other (lifted) foot round into a promenade position.

Who Did Well...

Claire and John pulled off the best Tango of the first series in the third week – but it wasn't enough to keep them in the competition. They scored 34 out of 40, putting them three points ahead of the eventual winners, Natasha and Brendan. In the second series, **Denise and Ian** were way ahead of all the competition, managing to score 35 points – that's six more than Jill and Darren. It just goes to show that the Tango is the odd one out of the ballroom section, calling on different talents than the more traditional numbers.

Cha Cha Cha

As the name suggests, the Cha Cha Cha is a little number which allows the dancers a bit of fun and a lot of flirting. But if you want to win, you have to watch those illegal moves...

The Cha Cha Cha is the cheeky younger cousin of the Rumba. They share similar step patterns, but the mood could not be more different. The Rumba is all about seduction – but the Cha Cha Cha is a fun, light-hearted dance in which the couple are expressing their delight in each other's company. The woman wiggles against the man, there's lots of hip action, even a little bit of bump and grind. But, for all that, there are strict rules. No matter how exciting the dance, some holds are just plain illegal – as Paul Killick was reminded when he swept Verona Joseph off her feet in the first-ever show, and was marked down accordingly.

History

During the 1940s, everyone was dancing the mambo – or at least having a go, as it was hard and fast and difficult to perfect. Orchestras started slowing the music down, and a new dance – a modified Rumba – was introduced to go with the easier pace. There's some debate about the origin of the name: some say it's a Haitian word for a bell-like musical instrument, others that it represents the sound of sandals slapping against the floor, as danced in Cuba. The Cha Cha Cha (or Cha Cha) as danced today was formulated by the dancers Pierre and Lavelle, who introduced the triple step that differentiates it from the Rumba.

Make-up. It's a Latin dance, so, of course, dark hair and tans are the order of the day. The hair is chic and simple, though, and the make-up softer than the more dramatic dances. Sparkly accessories add to the fun mood.

Dress. 'What aren't you wearing?' asked Bruce on more than one occasion, as the women's Cha Cha Cha dresses got shorter and smaller and more revealing. Sparkle and fringing adds to the sense of speed.

Feet. Feet are turned out and show a strong shape throughout the dance, rooting the couple to the floor whatever variations they go into.

Posture. Looser and more funky than most of the Latin dances, the Cha Cha Cha allows for a full range of postures and positions.

◗ Cuban Break
This is the second position of the Cuban break, a group of syncopated steps in which the dancers cross repeatedly in front of each other. The mood is light but sexy, even raunchy, with lots of hip action.

Arms. Lots of scope for movement with arms in the Cha Cha Cha, but the judges will always be looking for strong toning and a good finish in the fingers.

Legs. Leg lines between the two dancers are often parallel, forming some of the dance's most characteristic shapes. Toes are turned out, and there's a lot of hip action, shifting the weight from one foot to the other.

The Cha Cha Cha is a gay dance, in the old-fashioned sense of the word. It's sexy, but never in the same serious way as the Tango or the Rumba. It's important for me to see that the couple are enjoying themselves. I'm looking for a sense of spontaneity, although, of course, the steps are very difficult and have to be done precisely. It's extremely important that the dancers know where each other's body weight is going to be. You'll see all sorts of illegal moves in Cha Cha Cha – and that's fine for exhibition dances or shows, but in a competition you have to keep within the rules.

Cuban Break

As the dancers move around each other through the crossing sequence of the Cuban break, their legs remain parallel, the toes turned out. The arms are free and expressive.

New York

Cha Cha Cha originators Pierre and Lavelle discovered this move in the clubs of New York. The feet are turned out, and there's a strong 'V' shape through the bodies and outstretched arms.

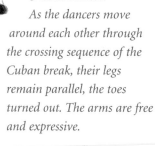

Open Hip Twist

The dancers prepare to go into the Hip Twist. Darren's weight is on the front leg, Lilia's is on the back as she prepares to 'twist' round into the first part of the rotation.

Aerial Rondé

Like the rondé in the Foxtrot, this is a circling movement of the leg. Beginners are encouraged to keep the rondé low and close to the floor. As dancers become more advanced, the leg moves higher.

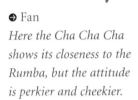

Fan

Here the Cha Cha Cha shows its closeness to the Rumba, but the attitude is perkier and cheekier.

Wiggle

A typically cheeky Cha Cha Cha movement. The man's position is strong and macho, while the woman crouches at his feet, holds on to his hips and then wiggles her way up his legs.

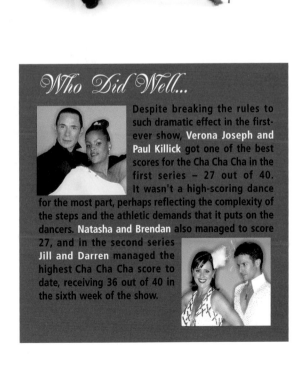

Who Did Well...

Despite breaking the rules to such dramatic effect in the first-ever show, **Verona Joseph and Paul Killick** got one of the best scores for the Cha Cha Cha in the first series – 27 out of 40. It wasn't a high-scoring dance for the most part, perhaps reflecting the complexity of the steps and the athletic demands that it puts on the dancers. **Natasha and Brendan** also managed to score 27, and in the second series **Jill and Darren** managed the highest Cha Cha Cha score to date, receiving 36 out of 40 in the sixth week of the show.

Quickstep

The Quickstep brings a smile to the face of any ballroom dancer. It's a fast and vibrant dance – not to mention being one of the simpler dances in the ballroom-dancing repertoire!

The fastest and happiest of the ballroom dances takes the couple speeding around the dance floor in a mixture of classic gliding movements and quick kicks and flicks. When it really gets going, the Quickstep can be as dramatic as the Tango, as athletic as the Cha Cha Cha – and it gives the ballroom brigade an opportunity to show off some pretty fancy footwork. Central to the Quickstep technique are the lockstep and the spin turn (see over), but there are also some showy elements of the Charleston and some pure showbiz kicks and drops thrown in there for good measure.

History

As the Foxtrot became the most popular dance of the 20s, bands started to play the music faster and faster, making it hard for all but the most skilful couples to keep up with them. And so the Quickstep was born, incorporating elements of the Charleston – another dance craze that was sweeping America and Europe at the time. English dancers Frank Ford and Molly Spain introduced it into competitions in 1927. Without the large open-leg movements of the Foxtrot, and with several syncopated steps, it soon became even more popular, and evolved into a dynamic dance of seemingly endless possibilities, incorporating hops, runs and rotation.

❯ Tiller Steps

A firm hold in the upper body allows the dancers to show off some fancy footwork made up of kicks and flicks (just like in the Jive). The weight rests lightly on their toes; they're almost floating.

Make-up. Like the Waltz, the women's look is classically glamorous, but here the hair is up. This focuses attention away from the head and on to the dress, which is where all the movement is coming from.

Arms. Back in the classic ballroom hold, the arms will remain in this basic firm position throughout the dance.

Dress. Floating chiffon panels and a layered skirt create a storm of movement around the dancers' legs, resulting in some dramatic effects (see over).

Legs. Rapid shifts of body weight give the Quickstep its skipping, tripping character. And there's far more running than in other ballroom dances.

Feet. Feet are light on the floor throughout the Quickstep, giving an impression of weightlessness. There's no stamping, just quick, light brushes and pivot turns.

Posture. The ballroom hold may be fundamentally the same, but the Quickstep allows the dancers a far greater range of movements. Suppleness is the name of the game.

Len Says...

The Quickstep is all about the mood. It's actually quite a simple dance and there aren't that many steps, so the dancers have to score points by getting the right mixture of smooth, gliding action and fast, showy kicks and flicks. When a Quickstep is done well, you should be watching it with a big grin on your face because it's so light and joyful. Anton and Erin are so light they're almost floating away.

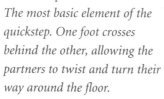

Lockstep

The most basic element of the quickstep. One foot crosses behind the other, allowing the partners to twist and turn their way around the floor.

Lockstep Sequence

The lockstep allows a wide variety of movement. Here Anton goes forward on to his left foot, Erin steps back on to her right and they both cross their feet with the other foot. That's the 'locking' action that gives the step its name.

Spin Turn

A turning action around each other and the woman brushes her right foot to her left foot, it touches and then comes back again as the man turns her.

Charleston

An element of the 1920s dance craze; here's the characteristic upwards flick of the foot.

Pivots

The dancers place their right feet between each others' legs as they turn continually around each other. The man's tails and the woman's skirt adds size and drama to the movement.

 Hinge Line with Kick

The couple's upper bodies separate like a door from a hinge, and the woman adds the final flourish by kicking her leg up, swinging from her left hip. See how the supporting foot is anchoring the movement under her skirt.

Who Did Well...

Almost everyone, apart from the decidedly earthbound Diarmuid Gavin, managed a creditable Quickstep; even Christopher Parker managed to score 23 out of 40. Natasha and Brendan got the highest marks of the first series (36), but they were pipped by Denise and Ian in the series-two final, who were only two points short of Quickstep perfection with 38 out of 40 points.

Samba

It's time to get down and party! This is the ultimate feel-good dance, where hot Latin rhythms and wild, seemingly unrestrained moves give a real flavour of Mardi Gras.

Welcome to Mardi Gras! The Samba is the most explosive and celebratory of all the ten dances, a wild collision of African steps and Brazilian rhythms that's become hugely popular all over the world. Essentially, it's a party dance that's been formalized for competitions, but even under the strict rules of ballroom it retains its unrestrained nature. Sexy costumes, bright colours and up-tempo music make it a favourite with audiences. But be warned: the judges are still looking for technique beneath the sizzling surface!

History

Like the Rumba, the Samba can be traced back to rhythms and steps brought to the New World by African slaves. The name derives from a Bantu word meaning to pray – and the dance and music originated as a way of calling forth the gods and inducing trance in worshippers. The steps were modified during the 19th century, transforming a wide range of steps into a partner dance that began to catch on in the USA and, by the 1920s, in Europe. Further boosts to the Samba's popularity came in the films of Fred Astaire and, in the 1940s, Carmen Miranda. Ballroom Samba, as danced competitively today, was formalized in 1956.

Make-up. The woman should look as if she's ready to go out to the carnival, but the make-up colours are definitely daytime rather than evening. Fake tan is an absolute must if you happen to be naturally pale-skinned like Lilia!

Arms. Where the Samba is concerned, 'straight is great' – not just to achieve the right lines, but in order to allow the dancers to communicate. Here the arms take the line to its ultimate extension.

Dress. Another case of 'less is more'. Women wear cut-away party outfits in bright colours, and there's less movement in the dress, allowing the focus to move to the limbs. If the man's in good shape, out comes the chest.

Feet. Fast and strong through the feet, the Samba demands absolute precision of movement, however extreme. It's important to use the feet as brakes in the fast turns and keep a balanced action throughout.

◔ Rolling Off the Arm

As well as celebrating movement and rhythm, the Samba should also tell a story. Here the woman turns off the man's arm, trying to get away – but he's going to pull her right back.

Legs. The focus tends to be on the straight leg, accentuating the rhythm of the music. The hips and legs should follow complex drum rhythms throughout the dance.

Posture. The woman is on show, but the man is doing all the leading, enabling her to achieve the rolls and freezes that make up many of the sequences. Backs are arched, limbs extended and toned.

❷ Open Rocks

The dancers express the rhythm of the Samba in a series of 'rocks' – strong leg and hip movements – that are executed in a loose (open) hold. Lilia has just flipped her hips across; Darren reflects the line in his position.

➔ Volta

This is a crossing action of the feet which can be danced either in a straight line (as demonstrated) or in a circle or on the spot.

➔ Shadow Botafogo

What's a botafogo? It's a move that was invented and popularized at Botafogo Bay in Brazil. The dancer settles on to the straight leg, then goes into a plié on the soft knee. It's called 'shadow' because the two dancers reflect each other's movements.

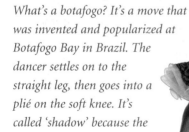

➔ Shadow Volta

Just like the volta above, but this time in shadow position, with both dancers facing forward rather than facing each other.

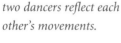

● Botafogos Side by Side
The same combination of straight leg and soft knee, but this time the dancers execute the move in the same direction, side by side.

➔ Runs
A travelling step that takes the couple across the floor, then adds an extra element by lifting the knee on the third beat. Another example of Samba storytelling – she's trying to run away, as he tries to keep her.

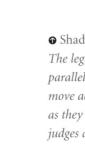

⬆ Shadow Roll
The legs at the back are perfectly parallel at this point, as the dancers move across the floor rotating the body as they go; this is the 'roll' that the judges are looking for.

● Promenade Runs
Another fast travelling step that contrasts well with other promenade positions across the ten dances. Here in the Samba it's fast and sassy; note how Lilia's and Darren's toes are pointed towards each other at the front.

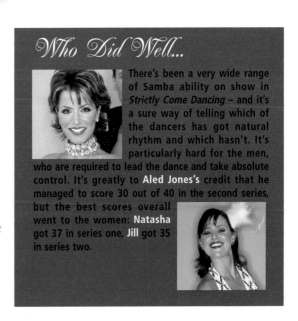

Who Did Well...

There's been a very wide range of Samba ability on show in *Strictly Come Dancing* – and it's a sure way of telling which of the dancers has got natural rhythm and which hasn't. It's particularly hard for the men, who are required to lead the dance and take absolute control. It's greatly to **Aled Jones's** credit that he managed to score 30 out of 40 in the second series, but the best scores overall went to the women: Natasha got 37 in series one, **Jill** got 35 in series two.

Viennese Waltz

The Viennese Waltz is an elegant, stately dance that is familiar to many. With mercifully few steps, it is simpler than the English Waltz, but still demands a sense of control – and direction!

The 'quick' or Viennese Waltz (as distinguished from the 'slow' or English Waltz) is all based on rotation – the couple simply spins around the floor in 3:4 time. And that, in a nutshell, is that. There are few steps, no jerkiness, no attitudes, just the elegance of continued turns, either travelling or stationary. It's a chance for dancers to show that they're in tune as a couple, that they know how to use the floor and that they can negotiate their way in between other moving dancers without causing a pile-up – which they certainly didn't manage to do in the first series!

History

The faster version of the waltz (120–180 beats per minute), known as the Viennese, is probably closer in spirit to the dance's peasant origins. Its main antecedent is the Austrian Landler, a dance in triple time, which featured a great deal of hopping and stamping. Moving into the ballrooms of the 19th century, it became faster and more refined, attracting the attention of the great composers of the day including, of course, Johann Strauss. Falling out of favour in the early 20th century, it was revived in the 30s, when it stirred nationalist sentiments during the rise of Nazism, and has remained a dance-floor staple ever since.

Make-up. Once again, elegance and simplicity is key. Erin's hair is up again; with all the turning that this waltz entails, she can't have it flicking in her face all the time.

Arms. The classic ballroom hold remains absolutely, firmly in place throughout the dance. It's vital that the man can steer his partner wherever they need to go, using pressure at the contact points without breaking step.

Dress. As in all the 'smooth' ballroom dances, the skirt is full and flowing to emphasize the grace of the turn, while floating panels exaggerate the movement. Dark colours and sparkling stones give a nocturnal feel.

Feet. The Viennese Waltz is all in the feet. The feet must be absolutely perfect, toned and precise in movement.

✪ Fleckerl
The classic spin of the Viennese Waltz can be done either way ('natural' or 'reverse') and brings the dancers to their maximum velocity.

Legs. Despite the apparent simplicity of the dance, the legs have to be in the right place at the right time, with each partner's knees set slightly to the side of the other's in order to avoid knocking them.

Posture. Pretty much straight up and down for this dance; it's all about the turns!

There's not much to say about the Viennese Waltz except that it's what most people think of when they think of ballroom dancing – it's exhausting, like doing the 100m sprint, circling. This is one that we'd nearly always watch being performed in a group, rather than marking individual couples. There's nothing better than seeing a group of dancers all spinning around in one direction, then doing a quick contra check before they fleckerl off the other way. This is the dance that you'd do to all those classic Strauss waltzes, like the Blue Danube. It's the most limited of all the ten dances in terms of steps, so the hold and the technique have to be absolutely flawless.

Natural Turn

The natural turn is a moving step turning to the right, and on the third step both parties close their feet.

⬇ ↘ Reverse Turn

The reverse turn is also a travelling step, but on the third step of the reverse turn, the man crosses his left foot in front of his right foot; on the sixth step, the woman crosses her left foot in front of her right foot, and this movement is continued to turn to the left.

Fleckerl

The fleckerl is a stationary turn in which the couple spin on the spot rather than travelling across the floor. Here, Anton and Erin demonstrate both natural and reverse fleckerls.

 Contra Check

In order for the couple to change direction from natural to reverse, they need to start dancing the contra check, in which they suddenly stop moving one way and start going the other.

Who Did Well...

The group Viennese-waltz event in the first series was a bit of a pile-up, as the couples careered into each other, lost their footing and started giggling. Nobody emerged from that episode with much credit – and so for the second series, there was a great deal more emphasis on navigation as the couples sailed round the Blackpool dance floor. This time at least one couple passed with flying colours, namely **Denise and Ian**.

Be Your Own Judge

		Darren & Lilia	Patsy & Anton	Colin & Erin	Siobhan & Matthew	James & Camilla	Gloria & Darren	
Show 1	Your Score							
	Judges' Score							
Show 2	Your Score							
	Judges' Score							
Show 3	Your Score							
	Judges' Score							
Show 4	Your Score							
	Judges' Score							
Show 5	Your Score							
	Judges' Score							
Show 6	Your Score							
	Judges' Score							

	Will & Hanna	Jaye & Andrew	Bill & Karen	Fiona & Brendan	Dennis & Izabela	Zoe & Ian	Knocked Out

Be Your Own Judge

		Jane & Bill	Darren & Lilia	Patsy & Anton	Colin & Erin	Siobhan & Matthew	James & Camilla	Gloria & Darren	
Show 7	Your Score									
	Judges' Score									
Show 8	Your Score									
	Judges' Score									
Show 9	Your Score									
	Judges' Score									
The Final	Your Score									
	Judges' Score									
	Your Score									
	Judges' Score									

	Will & Hanna	Jaye & Andrew	Bill & Karen	Fiona & Brendan	Dennis & Izabela	Zoe & Ian	Knocked Out
							Winner

Next Steps

IMPERIAL SOCIETY OF TEACHERS OF DANCING

The ISTD Dance Examinations Board offers dance examinations in 15 dance genres, including Modern Ballroom and Latin-American. Teachers who offer their examinations can be found throughout the UK and overseas. If you can't find a teacher in your area they will provide a list of schools, just email: education@istd.org.

Imperial House
22–6 Paul Street
London EC2A 4QE

Tel: +44 (0)20 7377 1577
Website: www.istd.org

NATIONAL ASSOCIATION OF TEACHERS OF DANCING

The National Association offers classes and examinations in the following branches: Ballroom, Latin-American, Disco, Street, Rock 'n' Roll, Country & Western Line Dancing, Salsa, Mambo, Merengue, Classical & Modern Sequence. Contact them for more information.

NATD
44–7 The Broadway
Thatcham
Berkshire RG19 3HP

Tel: + 44 (0) 1635 868888
Website: www.natd.org.uk

INTERNATIONAL DANCE TEACHERS' ASSOCIATION

Log on to their website to find a dance teacher or course near you – all over the world – or contact them direct and they will send you a free and comprehensive list of IDTA-registered teachers in your area.

**International House
76 Bennett Road
Brighton
East Sussex BN2 5JL**

**Tel: +44 (0)1273 685652
Website: www.idta.co.uk**

UNITED KINGDOM ALLIANCE OF PROFESSIONAL TEACHERS OF DANCING

Log on to their website or contact the UKA direct for guidance on finding your nearest registered dance teacher.

**Centenary House
38–40 Station Road
Blackpool
FY4 1EU**

**Tel: +44 (0)1253 408828
Website: www.ukadance.co.uk**